To bid or not to bid, that was the question.
"Tis nobler to pass," was Eddie's suggestion

To preempt perchance, maybe to double
"Both of those calls," he said, "will spell trouble."

I ran down the list of the bids that I knew
And Eddie admitted I knew quite a few.

The problem was clearly just evaluation,
Choosing the right bid for each situation.

How often a novice and even a master
will suffer the slings of a bidding disaster.

That's why, I must tell you, this book is a pleasure.
The bidding tips herein I view as a treasure.

And I have not a doubt, long before the last page
You'll know just why Kantar's my favorite bridge sage!

Phyllis Fein (1991)

OTHER BOOKS BY EDWIN B. KANTAR

KANTAR ON BRIDGE

A TREASURY
OF
BRIDGE TIPS

To Mildred, and to all the good times we had. Love, Eddie Kantar

HOWLAND PUBLISHING
514 West Bell Avenue
Santa Ana, CA 92707

10 9 8 7 6 5 4 3 2 1

Edwin B. Kantar, Post Office Box 427, Venice, CA 90294.

Address publisher inquiries to:

Howland Publishing, 514 West Bell Avenue, Santa Ana, CA 92707.

ISBN: 0-9630970-0-8

INTRODUCTION

The book you are holding is not meant for beginners, nor is it aimed at experts. It is directed at players somewhere between these extremes who would like to improve their game substantially. Could this be you?

Let it be said at trick one that few of these tips apply 100% of the time. Bidding tips seldom do. You must factor in variables such as the strength of your opponents, the strength of your partner, the strength of the intermediate cards in your long suit and the vulnerability, etc. However, an average player (your partner) should be able to improve his or her game at least 25% by following these tips.

The reader is going to have to put a certain amount of trust (some would call it blind faith) in me. Most of these tips, a few controversial, come with examples but not always with every supporting reason. If every reason were always listed, you would be clutching a tome. The asterisk preceding a tip means that it is a controversial tip, — that is, one which some experts, however misguided, may not see in exactly the same light as I do. Nonetheless, I stand by my asterisks ... period!

A "must do" is to be aware of the chapter title in which a tip appears. For example, if the chapter is entitled, "When You Are a Passed Hand," those words will not appear before every tip. You must add them mentally to the tip for it to make sense.

In the interest of brevity, certain abbreviations are used. The " + " means "or more." Thus, "11 + HCP" means "11 or more high card points." "Strong suit" refers to any suit headed by three of the top five honors, the kinds of suits your opponents always hold.

It might be wise to take these tips in small doses and try to absorb the messages. That is not to say that you should accept every tip or idea presented. If you play a different system, are comfortable with it, *and it works*, by all means disregard the tip. If it isn't broken, don't fix it.

Finally, I would like to thank Ron Garber, Norm Cressy and Allan Falk for looking over the manuscript (including inserting 12,800 commas) and making my sentences intelligible. I also want to thank Jacqui DeRouin. Without her sense of humor and computer expertise, this book would never have seen the light of day.

Eddie Kantar
Santa Monica, CA

Table of Contents

THE OPENING BID - Tips 1-28

1. Before opening the bidding with a distributional hand, prepare your various rebids. Assume partner will respond in your shortest suit ... he always does.

2. Deduct one point for any singleton jack, queen or king, as well as QJ doubleton. If you still have 12 points including distribution, open; otherwise, pass.

*3. With two five card suits, open the bidding in the higher ranking suit regardless of relative suit strength. However, with specifically five clubs and five spades, open 1♣ if (1) the hand is strong enough to jump shift; (2) the hand is *minimum* and the *spades* are *weak*.

You hold: (a) ♠A4 ♥87654 ♦AKJ87 ♣2
(b) ♠AKJ94 ♥43 ♦2 ♣AKQJ4
(c) ♠J8732 ♥A2 ♦2 ♣AK1087
(d) ♠AQ987 ♥32 ♦2 ♣AQ1043

With (a), open 1♥, the higher ranking suit.
With (b), open 1♣; you are strong enough to jump shift.
With (c), open 1♣; the hand is minimum and the spades are weak.
With (d), open 1♠; the hand is minimum, but the spades are strong.

*4. With 4-4 in the minors, open the stronger suit. Remember, partner may be on lead. If the suits are of near equal strength, open 1♦.

You hold: (a) ♠A4 ♥J54 ♦KQJ9 ♣Q876
(b) ♠A4 ♥J54 ♦Q876 ♣KQJ9
(c) ♠A3 ♥J54 ♦QJ104 ♣AJ97

With (a), open 1♦.
With (b), open 1♣.
With (c), open 1♦.

5. A short diamond is opened with *one* hand pattern: 4-4-3-2. In addition, the hand must be either too weak or too strong to open 1NT.

As dealer, you hold: (a) ♠AQ54 ♥AQ54 ♦J54 ♣32
(b) ♠AQ54 ♥AQ54 ♦A87 ♣98

With (a), open 1♦.
With (b), open 1NT.

6. Do not open the bidding 1♣ holding a singleton or doubleton club ... ever!

7. With 4-3-3-3 distribution (the four card suit a major) and a hand either too weak or too strong to open 1NT, open 1♣, not 1♦. (See tip #5)

You hold: ♠AJ8 ♥KQ87 ♦AKJ ♣J87. Open 1♣.

8. It is permissible to open 1NT or 2NT with a small doubleton; however, if your nerves are shot, have stoppers in the other three suits.

9. With four clubs and four spades, a hand strong enough to open 1NT but *no* stopper in *either* red suit, open 1♣.

You hold: ♠AKJ4 ♥32 ♦876 ♣AKJ4. Open 1♣.

10. With four diamonds and four spades, a hand strong enough to open 1NT, but no stopper in either unbid suit, open 1♦.

You hold: ♠AKQ4 ♥654 ♦AQJ8 ♣42.

Open 1♦. If partner responds 1♥, rebid 1♠. If partner responds 2♣, rebid 2♠.

*11. With a balanced hand containing five hearts and 15-16 HCP, open 1NT. With 17 HCP, open 1♥.

You hold: (a) ♠A4 ♥KJ876 ♦AJ7 ♣Q108
(b) ♠A4 ♥KJ987 ♦AQ9 ♣K106

With (a), open 1NT. If you open 1♥ and partner responds either 1♠ or 1NT, you have a tough rebid problem.
With (b), open 1♥. If partner responds 1♠, jump to 2NT. If partner responds 1NT, raise to 2NT. If partner responds 2♣ or 2♦, jump to 3NT.

2

*12. With a balanced hand containing five spades and 15-16 HCP, open 1♠ unless the spades are emaciated. If they are, open 1NT.

You hold: (a) ♠J7654 ♥AQ2 ♦KJ10 ♣AJ.
           (b) ♠KQ876 ♥A2 ♦AJ4 ♣Q98

With (a), bid 1NT. You want the lead to come up to this hand.
With (b), open 1♠.

Tips 11 and 12 assume a 15-17 1NT opening range. If you play 16-18, only 16 point hands with five hearts and 16 point hands with weak spades open 1NT.

13. Even if you play that a 2NT opening bid shows 22-24 HCP, open 2NT with 21 plus a five card suit - *any* five card suit.

14. With 3-1-4-5 or 1-3-4-5 distribution, open 1♦ if the diamonds are strong, the clubs weak and the hand has less than 17 HCP.

You hold: (a) ♠A54 ♥3 ♦AQJ9 ♣Q8765
           (b) ♠A54 ♥3 ♦AQJ9 ♣AQ876
           (c) ♠A54 ♥3 ♦K1032 ♣AQJ87.

With (a), open 1♦.
With (b), open 1♣; you are strong enough to reverse.
With (c), open 1♣; the diamonds are not strong enough.

15. With any 4-3-3-3 distribution, open with 13+ HCP; pass with 11 HCP or less. With exactly 12 HCP, open if the hand has good intermediates; otherwise, pass.

You hold: (a) ♠KJ8 ♥A632 ♦K43 ♣Q32
           (b) ♠KJ84 ♥A63 ♦Q43 ♣Q76
           (c) ♠KJ10 ♥A1032 ♦K82 ♣J104

With (a), open 1♣ (13 HCP).
With (b), pass (12 HCP and no intermediates).
With (c), open 1♣ (12 HCP but good intermediates).

16. With any 4-4-3-2 distribution, open with 12+ HCP; pass with less.

3

You hold: (a) ♠KJ84 ♥72 ♦AQ54 ♣Q43
         (b) ♠72 ♥KJ84 ♦Q43 ♣AJ76

With (a), open 1♦.
With (b), pass.

17. With three four card suits plus a singleton, open 1♦ unless the singleton is in diamonds, then open 1♣.

18. With 4-4-4-1 distribution, open with 11 + HCP with a *red* singleton, 12 + HCP with a *black* singleton. Hands with red singletons are easier to rebid. Also, remember to deduct one point for a singleton jack, queen or king.

You hold: (a) ♠AQ76 ♥3 ♦KJ104 ♣J965
         (b) ♠3 ♥KJ104 ♦AQ76 ♣J965.

With (a), open 1♦.
With (b), pass.

19. With any 5-3-3-2 distribution, open with 12 + HCP; pass with less.

20. With any 5-4-2-2 distribution, open with 12 + HCP, pass with less. However, if *all* 11 HCP are in the two long suits, and the five card suit is strong, open.

You hold: (a) ♠AQ876 ♥K4 ♦Q875 ♣42
         (b) ♠AQ1054 ♥32 ♦KQ54 ♣32.

With (a), pass.
With (b), open 1♠.

21. With any 5-4-3-1 distribution, open with 12 + HCP; pass with 10 or fewer HCP. With exactly 11 HCP, open if the five card suit is strong. If the five card suit is weak, consider the rebid problem if partner responds in your *short* suit. If the rebid will be awkward, pass; if it won't, open.

You hold: (a) ♠A43 ♥KQ1087 ♦2 ♣Q765
         (b) ♠A43 ♥K8765 ♦A876 ♣2
         (c) ♠A43 ♥K8765 ♦2 ♣A876

With (a), open 1♥; your five card suit is strong.
With (b), open 1♥; you have an easy 2♦ rebid if partner responds 2♣.
With (c), pass; you have an awkward rebid if partner responds 2♦. Avoid rebidding weak five card suits, and your only possible rebid is 2♥. (If you think that there are other possible rebids, don't mention them in public.)

*22. With any 5-5 distribution, open with 11 + HCP, pass with less. However, with exactly 10 HCP, open the higher ranking suit if:
(1) the suit is a major;
(2) the suit contains three honor cards;
(3) *all* 10 HCP are in the two long suits.

You hold: (a) ♠AQ654 ♥KJ543 ♦54 ♣3
(b) ♠AQ1087 ♥KJ763 ♦54 ♣2

With (a), pass; your spades are not strong enough.
With (b), open 1♠; your spades are strong enough.

23. With a six card suit, open with 11 + HCP; pass with less. However, with any 6-4 distribution, open with 10 HCP if the six card suit is strong (three of the top five honors).

You hold: (a) ♠4 ♥KQ8765 ♦A76 ♣Q54
(b) ♠4 ♥A97654 ♦KJ75 ♣Q2
(c) ♠4 ♥AQ10543 ♦KJ75 ♣32

With (a), open 1♥; you have 11 HCP.
With (b), pass; with 10 HCP and 6-4 distribution, you need a stronger six card suit.
With (c), open 1♥; your hearts are strong enough.

24. With 5-6 distribution in adjacent suits, the five card suit being higher ranking, open the six card suit with 14 + HCP. With 10-13 HCP, open the five card suit; with less, pass.

You hold: (a) ♠3 ♥AQJ76 ♦KJ8743 ♣2
(b) ♠3 ♥AQJ76 ♦AQJ876 ♣2
(c) ♠3 ♥KQ876 ♦A98765 ♣2

With (a), open 1♥.
With (b), open 1♦.
With (c), pass.

25. Add one point to any hand that has three tens each connected with a higher honor, or two 109 combinations in four card suits or longer.

You hold: (a) ♠AJ10 ♥AJ104 ♦Q104 ♣876
          (b) ♠A10932 ♥A1094 ♦A32 ♣3

Both of these hands count to 13 points, excluding distributional considerations.

26. Unless you fear the heavens will part, open 1♥ or 1♠ in third or fourth seat with a strong four card suit and a minimum hand.

You hold: ♠54 ♥AKJ10 ♦10987 ♣A104.

In fourth seat, open 1♥. If you play four card majors, open 1♥ in any seat.

27. If you feel the decision is close about whether or not to open, let the intermediate cards in the long suits be the deciding factor. (See tips 21, 22 and 23)

*28. With a broken six card minor and 15 HCP, open 1NT if you have stoppers in the other three suits.

You hold: ♠K4 ♥K4 ♦KJ8 ♣AJ7654.

Live a little, open 1NT.

THE FIRST RESPONSE - Tips 29-40

*29. Assume partner opens 1♣ and you have four diamonds along with a four card major. With less than 11 HCP, respond in the major. With 11 or more HCP, respond in your stronger suit. You are strong enough to bid the other one later, if necessary.

You hold: (a) ♠A875 ♥76 ♦KQ76 ♣654
           (b) ♠A875 ♥76 ♦AKJ9 ♣654

North	East	South (you)	West
1♣	Pass	?	

With (a), respond 1♠. You have fewer than 11 HCP.
With (b), respond 1♦. You are strong enough to bid both suits if necessary.

*30. Do not respond in a suit that has four small cards when you have an opening bid or better. There may be a slam and you could wind up in the wrong suit.

You hold: ♠AKQ10 ♥9432 ♦AJ4 ♣J8

North	East	South (you)	West
1♣	Pass	?	

Respond 1♠. Trust me.

31. With 4-4 in the majors, respond 1♥ to a minor suit opening bid. With 5-5, respond in the higher ranking suit first.

You hold: (a) ♠AJ98 ♥Q765 ♦54 ♣J98
           (b) ♠Q7654 ♥AKJ105 ♦54 ♣3

North	East	South (you)	West
1♣	Pass	?	

With (a), respond 1♥.
With (b), respond 1♠.

32. With a five card major and 5 HCP or a six card major with 4 HCP, do not pass a minor suit opening bid if second hand passes.

You hold: (a) ♠K9765 ♥Q87 ♦543 ♣32
(b) ♠KJ8765 ♥43 ♦54 ♣875

North	East	South (you)	West
1♣	Pass	?	

Respond 1♠ with both hands - in an audible voice!

33. With a five card minor and a four card major, respond in the longer suit with 11 + HCP. With less, respond in the major.

You hold: (a) ♠AK32 ♥42 ♦J8765 ♣32
(b) ♠AK32 ♥42 ♦A10765 ♣32

North	East	South (you)	West
1♣	Pass	?	

With (a), respond 1♠.
With (b), respond 1♦.

34. With game going responding hands, respond in your longer suit first. Reread this one.

35. In some systems, a two-over-one response is a game force. In others, it promises one more bid; in still others, it does not promise another bid if partner makes a minimum rebid. It behooves you to know which of these methods you and your partner are playing!

36. In most systems a two-over-one response followed by a rebid of the same suit is not considered forcing. The sequence shows 8-10 HCP with a strong suit and is one of the rare times responder can venture into the two level with fewer than 10 HCP.

You hold: (a) ♠753 ♥64 ♦AKJ1074 ♣32
(b) ♠753 ♥64 ♦K87654 ♣KQ

North	East	South (you)	West
1♥	Pass	?	

With (a), respond 2♦ and rebid 3♦, not forcing, but invitational to 3NT.

8

With (b), respond 1NT with an eight count. Your diamond suit is not strong enough to bid at the two level.

37. With 4-3-3-3 distribution and 6-7 HCP plus three card support for partner's major suit opening, respond 1NT. With the same distribution and 8-10 HCP, raise partner to the two level. However, if *all* of the points are in partner's suit, raise regardless.

You hold: (a) ♠Q54 ♥J876 ♦Q87 ♣Q98
            (b) ♠AQ10 ♥8765 ♦543 ♣1087
            (c) ♠975 ♥KQ4 ♦A876 ♣432

North	East	South (you)	West
1♠	Pass	?	

With (a), respond 1NT to slow down the auction with this piece of cheese.
With (b), raise to 2♠. All of your strength is in partner's suit.
With (c), raise to 2♠, more encouraging than 1NT.

38. A direct *natural* response of either 2NT or 3NT *denies* a singleton. A 1NT response may contain a singleton - or even a void!

You hold: (a) ♠3 ♥AQ87 ♦KQ42 ♣K1087
            (b) ♠ — ♥K876 ♦Q10876 ♣Q543

North	East	South (you)	West
1♠	Pass	?	

With (a), respond 2♣. Do not even think of responding 2NT. You can bid notrump later if you wish.
With (b), respond 1NT.

39. A 2♥ response to a 1♠ opening bid promises at least five hearts. A 2♣ or 2♦ response to a major suit opening bid can be made on a four card suit.

40. In competition, a response of either 2♥ or 2♠ promises at least a five card suit. With a four card major, think "negative double."

You hold: (a) ♠32 ♥AJ1043 ♦42 ♣KQJ4
         (b) ♠32 ♥KQ74 ♦432 ♣AK98

North	East	South (you)	West
1♠	2♦	?	

With (a), bid 2♥. You have your five card suit, and you have your 10 HCP.
With (b), double. More on this in the chapter on Negative Doubles.

OPENER'S REBID - 41-64

41. After a two level response, a new suit by the opener is forcing.

You hold: ♠AK1065 ♥4 ♦AK74 ♣A108

> South (you)   North
> 1♠   2♣
> ?

Rebid 2♦. Do not crowd the auction with a jump shift.

42. After a single raise, a new suit is forcing.

You hold: ♠87 ♥AQ5 ♦A4 ♣AK9874

> South (you)   North
> 1♣   2♣
> ?

Bid 2♥, forcing, If partner rebids 3♣, bid 3♦, forcing. What you are hoping is that partner with a spade stop will bid 3NT. Bidding on after a single raise shows 16 + HCP. It does *not* mean that you are running away from a short club opening.

43. Avoid rebidding weak five card suits. Look for something else.

You hold: ♠K4 ♥AK3 ♦432 ♣K8765

> South (you)   North
> 1♣   1♦/♥/♠
> ?

If partner responds 1♦ or 1♠, rebid 1NT. If partner responds 1♥, raise to 2♥. If your religion forbids three card trump raises, rebid 1NT over 1♥ and consider attending a different church.

For non-churchgoers: With 4-4 in the minors, 3-2 in the majors, and a hand not strong enough to open 1NT, open the stronger minor. If partner responds in the doubleton suit, rebid 1NT; if partner responds in the tripleton suit, raise. However, if the doubleton is strong and the support marginal (Qxx or worse), rebid 1NT.

You hold: (a) ♠AK4 ♥54 ♦AJ105 ♣J987
         (b) ♠1043 ♥AQ ♦AJ105 ♣Q987

South (you)	North
1♦	1♥/♠

With either hand, bid 1NT over a 1♥ response. With (a), raise 1♠
to 2♠; with (b), rebid 1NT over a 1♠ response.

44. Treat a five card suit headed by 100 or 150 honors as if it were a
six card suit.

You hold: ♠32 ♥876 ♦A54 ♣AKQJ9.

Open 1♣ and rebid 2♣ over any one level response.

45. With a minimum hand and 2-2-5-4 distribution, open 1♦ and
rebid 2♣ over a major suit response. However, if the major suit
doubletons are strong, rebid 1NT.

You hold: (a) ♠94 ♥K3 ♦AJ987 ♣KQ98
         (b) ♠AQ ♥K3 ♦Q8765 ♣Q876

South (you)	North
1♦	1♥
?	

With (a), rebid 2♣.
With (b), rebid 1NT.

46. With 3-1-5-4 or 1-3-5-4 distribution, open 1♦. If partner responds
in the singleton suit, rebid 2♣, not 1NT.

You hold: ♠J ♥A43 ♦J10765 ♣AK54

South (you)	North
1♦	1♠
?	

Rebid 2♣, not 1NT.

47. With 3-1-5-4 or 1-3-5-4 distribution, open 1♦. If partner responds in your three card major, raise with 11-14 HCP. With 15-17 HCP, rebid 2♣ and then support the major.

You hold: (a) ♠3 ♥A76 ♦KQ765 ♣QJ98
           (b) ♠3 ♥AK6 ♦KQ765 ♣QJ98

> **South** (you)   **North**
> 1♦   1♥
> ?

With (a), raise to 2♥.
With (b), rebid 2♣ and then support hearts.

*48. With 4-3-2-4 or 4-3-4-2 distribution and 12-14 HCP, open one of the minor. If partner responds 1♥, rebid 1♠. However, if the hearts are strong and the spades weak, raise to 2 ♥.

You, South, hold: (a) ♠AJ76 ♥K54 ♦32 ♣AJ98
                  (b) ♠10765 ♥AK4 ♦32 ♣AQ98

> **South** (you)   **North**
> 1♣   1♥
> ?

With (a), rebid 1♠.
With (b), rebid 2♥.

Some players always rebid 1♠, but limiting your hand with a single raise will seldom get you in trouble. Rebidding 1♠ and later supporting hearts shows extra values, distributional or otherwise, in certain sequences. (See next tip.).

49. Indirect support is stronger than direct support. Indirect support at the two level is invitational; at the three level, forcing. Both show three card support.

You hold: ♠AK87 ♥AJ4 ♦4 ♣K10543

(a) **South** (you)   **North**
   1♣   1♥
   1♠   1NT
   ?

Bid 2♥, invitational, 13-15 HCP and a singleton diamond.

(b) **South** (you)   **North**
   1♣   1♥
   1♠   2NT
   ?

Bid 3♥, forcing.

50. Return preference to a major suit after a 1NT response usually shows a doubleton.

South (you)   **North**
   1♥   1NT
   2♣   2♥

Partner is likely to have two hearts, not three.

51. A jump shift followed by a simple return to partner's original suit shows three card support, not four.

South holds: ♠AJ4 ♥2 ♦AJ842 ♣AK95

South (you)   **North**
   1♦   1♠
   3♣   3♦
   3♠

Your bidding shows *three* card spade support. With four spades, either jump in spades directly, make a splinter jump (more about that later) or jump in spades later.

52. Anytime you skip over two suits, including notrump, to rebid your original suit, you show a six card suit (or exceptionally five headed by 100 honors).

South (you)	North
1♣	1♦
2♣	

You have shown six clubs because you have skipped over 1♥, 1♠ and 1NT to rebid your suit.

53. Rebidding a suit three times tends to show a seven card suit or, at the very least, a strong six carder.

You hold: ♠4 ♥AJ97542 ♦K75 ♣Q4

South (you)	North
1♥	1♠
2♥	2NT
?	

Rebid 3♥, not forcing, implying a seven card suit with a weak opening bid.

*54. With a six card minor and three card support for partner's major, rebid the minor if the suit is strong. If the suit is weak and the support is strong, raise the major. With marginal hands, rebid the minor if you are the stronger declarer, raise the major if partner is. (But don't tell partner why you are always rebidding your suit!)

You hold: (a) ♠K43 ♥54 ♦AQJ987 ♣Q4
          (b) ♠KQ4 ♥A2 ♦J98765 ♣Q4
          (c) ♠QJ5 ♥2 ♦AJ9754 ♣A98

South (you)	North
1♦	1♠
?	

With (a), rebid 2♦.
With (b), raise to 2♠.
With (c), raise to 2♠ with a good partner; rebid 2♦ with your regular one.

55. With a six card minor, 16-17 HCP, 6-3-2-2 distribution and stoppers in the unbids, rebid 2NT over a one level response rather than make a jump rebid.

You hold: ♠54 ♥AQ ♦AKJ1043 ♣K43.

South (you)	North
1♦	1♠
?	

Rebid 2NT rather than 3♦. Had partner responded 1♥, rebid 3♦ — no spade stop.

56. With three four card suits and a singleton diamond, open 1♣ and rebid 1♥ over a 1♦ response. If you rebid 1♠, you deny four hearts.

You hold: ♠AJ98 ♥J876 ♦2 ♣AK76

South (you)	North
1♣	1♦
?	

Rebid 1♥. If partner has four spades, you will hear about it ... right now.

57. With 5-4-4-0 distribution, open 1♠. If partner responds 2♣, your void suit, rebid 2♥, not 2♦. If you rebid 2♦, you deny four hearts.

 You hold: ♠AJ987 ♥K876 ♦AQ76 ♣ —

South (you)	North
1♠	2♣
?	

Rebid 2♥.

58. With a six card major and a four card minor, rebid the major with 11-13 HCP; rebid the minor with 14-16 HCP.

You hold: (a) ♠2 ♥AQ10543 ♦K4 ♣Q876
           (b) ♠2 ♥AQ8765 ♦K4 ♣AQ76

South (you)	North
1♥	1♠
?	

With (a), rebid 2♥.
With (b), rebid 2♣.

59. With an *independent* six card major (one that can play opposite a singleton without shedding any tears), and a four card minor, rebid the major or jump in the major after a one- level response. Do not rebid the minor.

You hold: (a) ♠2 ♥KQJ1054 ♦K4 ♣Q876
(b) ♠2 ♥KQJ1054 ♦K4 ♣AJ94

South (you)	North
1♥	1NT
?	

With (a), rebid 2♥.
With (b), rebid 3♥

60. With 5-5 distribution and a forward going hand, open the higher ranking suit and rebid the lower ranking suit twice — even after partner gives you preference to your first suit.

Opener (you)	Responder		Opener	Responder
♠K8765	♠AJ		1♠	2NT
♥AK876	♥Q32		3♥	3♠
♦A2	♦KQ87		4♥	Pass
♣2	♣J853			

Responder is allowed to prefer spades with a strong doubleton rather than rebid 3NT with such weak clubs. Catering to this live possibility, opener rebids hearts. Sure enough, responder has two spades and three hearts. What did you expect? I made up the hand.

61. In a similar vein, with 5-4-2-2 distribution, do not necessarily insist upon your five card suit even after a preference.

You hold: ♠KQ765 ♥A1082 ♦AK ♣J4

South (you)	North
1♠	1NT
2♥	2♠
?	

Bid 2NT. Do not continue in spades! Partner probably has a doubleton spade. Rebid 2NT to show a forward going balanced hand. Partner knows you have five spades.

62. Now that you are getting into this, consider this distribution: 5-4-3-1. If you are strong enough, open the five card suit, rebid the four card suit and in some cases, rebid the three card suit next. What fun!

Opener (you)	Responder		Opener	Responder
♠ AQ432	♠ K5		1♠	1NT
♥ AJ4	♥ 107632		2♦	2♠
♦ AK75	♦ 32		?	
♣ 2	♣ A987			

Rebid 3♥, completing the picture of your hand. You cannot have four hearts in this sequence. If you rebid 3♥, partner raises to 4♥, and you are in the right contract. (See tip #57.)

*63. With 4-3-3-3 distribution, 12-14 HCP, (the four card suit a major), open 1♣ and rebid 1NT over a response in your three card suit. Do not rebid the major suit. Heresy!

You hold: (a) ♠ KJ76 ♥ A54 ♦ K54 ♣ Q54
(b) ♠ KJ76 ♥ A5 ♦ K54 ♣ Q543

South (you)	North
1♣	1♥
?	

With (a), rebid 1NT, not 1♠. This tip assumes a checkback method to determine whether opener has bypassed a four card major. With no checkback method, rebid 1♠.

With (b), rebid 1♠. When you rebid a major, you guarantee at least four clubs.

64. Bidding twice opposite a silent partner shows extra values, 15-17 HCP minimum. Bidding three times opposite a silent partner shows a hand in the 18-20 HCP range. Bidding four times opposite a silent partner hints strongly of a death wish!

RESPONDER'S REBID - Tips 65-80

65. A new suit by the responder is unlimited and forcing unless opener rebids 1NT.

66. If a one-level responder wishes to sign off, or make weak noises (6-9 HCP), the weak rebids are: pass, rebidding the original suit, returning to opener's first suit at the cheapest level, or 1NT.

You hold: (a) ♠87 ♥KQ9743 ♦J4 ♣J54
 (b) ♠87 ♥KJ842 ♦32 ♣QJ97
 (c) ♠3 ♥A7654 ♦Q54 ♣8743
 (d) ♠Q54 ♥KJ432 ♦2 ♣5432

North	South (you)
1♦	1♥
1♠	?

With (a), rebid 2♥ showing a *six* card suit or a strong five carder.
With (b), rebid 1NT. Do not even think of rebidding those seedy hearts!
With (c), return to 2♦. Partner must have diamond length. If you don't know why, check tip #5.
With (d), pass.

67. One level responding hands in the 10-12 HCP range are expected to make invitational rebids after opener shows a minimum hand. These invitational rebids are: 2NT or bidding at the three level any suit that has already been bid.

Opener	Responder	
1♦	1♥	
1♠	2NT	11-12 HCP, not forcing.
1♦	1♥	
1♠	3♥	9-11 HCP, plus a six card suit, not forcing.
1♦	1♥	
1♠	3♦	11-13 support points, not forcing.
1♦	1♥	
1♠	3♠	11-12 support points, not forcing.

19

68. After a one-level response, holding game-going values, rebid game if a major suit fit has been uncovered; rebid game with an independent major suit; or rebid 3NT, not 2NT, with a suitable hand.

You hold: (a) ♠76 ♥AKJ9843 ♦K4 ♣43
           (b) ♠AQ43 ♥AQ765 ♦65 ♣65
           (c) ♠654 ♥AK104 ♦832 ♣AQJ4

North	South (you)
1♦	1♥
1♠	?

With (a), bid 4♥; 3♥ is not forcing.
With (b), bid 4♠; 3♠ is not forcing.
With (c), bid 3NT; 2NT is not forcing.

69. When a one level responder wants to be in game but doesn't know which game, he bids a new suit to continue the force. If this new suit is the fourth suit, the bid may be completely artificial.

You hold: (a) ♠A4 ♥AKJ43 ♦J1054 ♣76
           (b) ♠A87 ♥AK765 ♦K2 ♣432

North	South (you)
1♦	1♥
1♠	?

With (a), bid 2♣. You are not sure whether this hand belongs in hearts , diamonds or even notrump. Bid 2♣ to find out more about partner's hand. Partner will not bid notrump without a club stopper. A three level jump to 3♦ or 3♥ would not be forcing.

With (b), bid 2♣. Once again, you cannot be sure whether this hand belongs in a suit or in notrump. Bid 2♣ to find out more about partner's hand.

*70. After fourth suit, any subsequent rebid at the three level is game forcing.

Opener	Responder	
1♦	1♥	
1♠	2♣	
2NT	3♣/♦/♥/♠	All forcing rebids.

Some play that 3♣ is not forcing in this sequence.

*71. After fourth suit, any subsequent rebid at the two level is invitational.

Opener	Responder	
1♦	1♥	
1♠	2♣	
2♦	2♥/♠/NT	All invitational rebids.

Some play that fourth suit is a game force. Others play that fourth suit is forcing to at least 2NT.

*72. After opener makes a jump rebid, a three level rebid in responder's original suit is forcing.

Opener	Responder		Opener	Responder
1♦	1♥		1♦	1♥
2NT	3♥ (forcing)		3♦	3♥ (forcing)

*73. When a three level rebid in responder's original suit is forcing, a jump to game instead shows a powerful six or seven card suit but little else.

You hold: (a) ♠74 ♥AQ8754 ♦93 ♣Q92
(b) ♠74 ♥AKJ1093 ♦2 ♣J876

North	South (you)
1♦	1♥
2NT	?

With (a), rebid 3♥, forcing, typically a six card suit.
With (b), jump to 4♥ to emphasize the quality of the suit. Armed with that specific knowledge, partner may be able to bid a slam.

74. Raising a second suit promises four card support.

Opener	Responder (you)
1♥	1♠
2♣	3♣

If you don't have at least four clubs, you had better have some pretty good reasons for your bid. One possibility is, "Sorry partner, I had one of my spades in with my clubs."

75. A direct response of 2NT not only shows 13-15 HCP but also denies a singleton. However, a 2NT *rebid,* which shows 11-12 HCP, may contain a singleton.

You hold: ♠KQ4 ♥K10543 ♦10 ♣K985

North	South (you)
1♦	1♥
1♠	?

Rebid 2NT, not forcing.

76. A direct response of 3NT shows 16-17 HCP and denies a singleton. A rebid of 3NT shows 13-15 HCP and may contain a singleton.

You hold: ♠AKQ ♥KQ875 ♦4 ♣J1054

North	South (you)
1♦	1♥
2♦	?

Rebid 3NT.

*77. Balanced hands in the 18-19 HCP range are too strong to respond 3NT directly. (See tip #75.) One solution is to respond 2NT, forcing, and then over any minimum rebid partner makes, rebid 4NT, invitational. Talk this one over!

You hold: ♠AJ4 ♥K87 ♦AQ5 ♣KJ54

North	South (you)
1♦	?

22

Respond 2NT, and rebid 4NT. What happens now is on partner's head. You have shown your hand to a "t".

78. Responding in a lower ranking suit and then rebidding a higher ranking suit shows 6-5 distribution.

You hold: ♠AJ876 ♥AK8765 ♦2 ♣3

North	South (you)
1♣	?

Plan to respond 1♥ and then bid and rebid spades.

79. Do not bid a new suit at the two level with less than 11 HCP unless partner rebids 1NT.

You hold: ♠54 ♥AJ843 ♦Q10876 ♣2

North	South (you)
1♣	1♥
1♠	?

Rebid 1NT. Do not rebid 2♦! You would be showing 11 + HCP.

80. After partner rebids 1NT, a new lower ranking suit is not forcing.

You hold: ♠54 ♥AJ843 ♦Q10876 ♣2

North	South (you)
1♣	1♥
1NT	?

Rebid 2♦, not forcing. Contrast this to your rebid on the previous tip.

THE JUMP SHIFT BY THE RESPONDER - Tips 81-89

81. Think of a jump shift as a slam invitation, not a slam force.

82. Most jump shifts contain 15-18 HCP, not 19 or more. Long suits and/or support for partner's suit take up the slack.

83. If you are lucky enough to have 19 or more HCP and partner opens, it is up to you to push to slam unless:

(1) The hand is misfitted.
(2) Two cashing aces are missing.
(3) You have two quick losers in one suit.
(4) You are missing one ace plus the king of trumps.
(5) You have an eight card trump fit and are missing one ace plus the trump queen.
(6) You have seen your partner play before.

84. A jump shift shows one of three types of hands:

(1) A one suited hand - six or more cards in the suit.
(2) A hand with *four* or more cards in partner's suit.
(3) A balanced hand with a five card suit.

You hold: (a) ♠AQJ987 ♥A2 ♦A54 ♣105
          (b) ♠AK876 ♥AQ43 ♦K4 ♣105
          (c) ♠AKJ87 ♥32 ♦AJ5 ♣K108

North	South (you)
1♥	?

With (a), jump to 2♠, intending to rebid the suit.
With (b), jump to 2♠, intending to return to hearts.
With (c), jump to 2♠, intending to rebid notrump.

85. Do *not* jump shift with a two or three-suited hand (unless one of the suits is partner's) regardless of strength.

You hold: (a) ♠AK76 ♥AQ76 ♦2 ♣AQ76
          (b) ♠AK87 ♥AK873 ♦2 ♣AJ2

North	South (you)
1♦	?

With both hands, respond 1♥. You do not have any of the three types of hands partner will be expecting for a jump shift. Discipline!

86. A jump shift in a major suit followed by a second jump in the same major to game, is a specialized sequence. It shows a solid seven or eight card suit *without* an outside ace. With a seven card suit, an outside king is necessary.

You hold: (a) ♠AKQJ876 ♥4 ♦43 ♣K65
　　　　　　 (b) ♠3 ♥AKQJ8763 ♦43 ♣62

North	South (you)
1♦	?

With (a), jump to 2♠ and then jump to 4♠
With (b), jump to 2♥ and then jump to 4♥.

87. After making a jump shift with primary support in partner's suit, return to partner's original suit if you have no side singleton. With a side singleton, bid the singleton suit instead. This is the Soloway Convention and it is quite popular.

You hold: (a) ♠AQ876 ♥AK65 ♦K4 ♣87
　　　　　　 (b) ♠AQ876 ♥AK65 ♦K42 ♣2

North	South (you)
1♥	2♠
2NT	?

With (a), rebid 3♥, denying a singleton.
With (b), rebid 3♣, showing four hearts plus a singleton club. (Remember, responder cannot have clubs. No jump shifts with two suited hands.)

88. Another specialized jump shift is a jump followed by a jump return to partner's first suit. This rebid shows excellent trumps and denies a control in the other two suits.

You hold: ♠AQJ76 ♥AKQ8 ♦54 ♣43

North	South (you)
1♥	?

Jump shift to 2♠ and then jump in hearts.

*89. A jump shift can be made on a four card suit providing responder has strong support for opener's first suit.

You hold: ♠K4 ♥2 ♦AKJ4 ♣A109765

North	South (you)
1♣	?

Jump to 2♦. This hand will be very difficult to describe if you begin with 1♦. A corollary to four card jump shifts is that opener must not raise directly without *four* card support. Not too many are in love with this corollary.

WHEN PARTNER MAKES A
JUMP SHIFT - Tips 90-93

90. Regardless of strength, it generally pays to make a minimum rebid allowing partner to describe the type of jump shift.

You hold: ♠A4 ♥65 ♦KJ4 ♣AQJ765

        South (you) **North**
        1♣   2♥
        ?

Although there is a certain slam or grand slam, bide your time with a 3♣ rebid. Find out more about partner's hand.

91. A jump rebid in your suit shows solidity; it does not show extra strength.

You hold: ♠2 ♥AKQJ76 ♦Q104 ♣876

        South (you) **North**
        1♥   2♠
        ?

Jump to 4♥ to show a solid suit.

*92. Do not rebid any suit that does not have an ace or a king. Partner does *not* have a second suit. Partner is more interested in learning *where* your strength is located.

You hold: ♠K7654 ♥AK10 ♦Q876 ♣2

        South (you) **North**
        1♠   3♣
        ?

Rebid 3♥ rather than 3♦. Partner cannot have four hearts, so there is no chance for a mix-up.

93. Before leaping to 4NT Blackwood, it pays to set the trump suit with a forcing raise at the three level, if possible.

You hold: ♠KJ42 ♥4 ♦AK763 ♣K54

South (you)	North
1♦	2♠
?	

Even though you are surely going to bid six or seven spades, set the suit with a raise to 3♠ before plunging into Blackwood. It helps when both partners know the agreed suit. Reread this.

WHEN YOU OVERCALL - Tips 94-107

94. A reasonable minimum for a one level overcall is a five card suit, at least 8 HCP, plus three of the top five honors in the suit.

You hold: (a) ♠87 ♥AQ1042 ♦543 ♣Q105
           (b) ♠87 ♥A7654 ♦Q43 ♣Q105

East	South (you)
1♦	?

With (a), overcall 1♥.
With (b), pass.

95. A two level overcall should have at least one ace or one king outside of the main suit. If it does not, chances are you have a weak jump overcall.

With neither side vulnerable, you hold:
           (a) ♠A4 ♥54 ♦AQJ1054 ♣876
           (b) ♠8 ♥875 ♦AQJ1054 ♣876

East	South (you)
1♣	?

With (a), overcall 1♦; you have an outside ace.
With (b), overcall 2♦; you have no outside ace or king.

96. The range of a one level overcall with a five card suit is 8-16 HCP and 5-3-3-2 distribution. With more, double, and then bid the five card suit.

You hold: (a) ♠KQJ ♥AK876 ♦Q54 ♣87
           (b) ♠AQ4 ♥AKJ54 ♦K54 ♣87

East	South (you)
1♣	?

With (a), overcall 1♥.
With (b), double and then bid hearts.

29

*97. A one level overcall by a non-passed hand can be made on a four card suit if:

(1) The suit contains three of the top five honors.
(2) The hand is worth an opening bid.
(3) The distribution does not qualify for a takeout double (either four cards in the opener's suit or lack of support for one of the unbid suits).
(4) Your voice doesn't crack.

You hold: (a) ♠AKJ4 ♥7432 ♦Q86 ♣32
           (b) ♠AKJ4 ♥7432 ♦A53 ♣32
           (c) ♠A1043 ♥7432 ♦Q2 ♣KQJ
           (d) ♠AKJ4 ♥32 ♦10987 ♣AJ3

East	South (you)
1♥	?

With (a), pass. Your suit is strong enough but your hand isn't.
With (b), overcall 1♠, perfect.
With (c), pass. Your suit is not strong enough and you are too weak to double lacking support in one of the unbid suits.
With (d), double. No need to overcall on a four card suit when your hand is suitable for a takeout double.

98. The most effective overcalls are those that take up the most bidding space from the opponents.

(a) East	South (you)
1♣	1♦

(b) East	South (you)
1♣	1♠

In (a), you have not made life difficult at all for West, who can still respond at the one level.
In (b), you have deprived West of a one level response in a red suit.

99. When your right hand opponent opens the bidding in one of your two five card suits and you have 10-14 HCP, bid your other five card suit at the one level if possible. If you must go to the two level, pass and await developments — unless you have strong intermediates in your second suit.

30

You hold: ♠4 ♥A10984 ♦43 ♣AK632

If your right hand opponent opens 1♣, overcall 1♥.
If your right hand opponent opens 1♥, pass. (Club spots are not good enough.)

100. With two five card suits and less than 19 HCP, overcall in the higher ranking suit. With more, double. This tip assumes you are not playing Michaels. (See tip #449.)

You hold: (a) ♠AQJ87 ♥5 ♦Q10876 ♣32
         (b) ♠AQJ87 ♥5 ♦AKJ87 ♣Q2
         (c) ♠AQJ87 ♥5 ♦AKJ87 ♣A2

East	South (you)
1♥	?

With (a) and (b), overcall 1♠.
With (c), double.

101. Avoid takeout doubles with six card major suits unless you have 16 + HCP. Avoid doubles with six card heart suits unless you have three card spade support.

You hold: (a) ♠3 ♥AKJ876 ♦AJ4 ♣KJ4
         (b) ♠AKJ876 ♥K54 ♦AJ4 ♣3

East	South (you)
1♣	?

With (a), overcall 1♥. Making a takeout double with a singleton spade (an unbid suit) is like crossing a busy intersection blindfolded ... maybe worse.
With (b), double. When you double with a six card spade suit, you can always correct to spades at the same level if partner gets rambunctious.

102. Vulnerable two level overcalls promise good suits plus opening bid or near opening bid values. Minor suit overcalls tend to show six card suits. An overcall of 2♥ is apt to be a five carder.

103. Whereas a vulnerable two level overcall generally shows three of the top five honors in the suit, a non-vulnerable two level overcall need not be quite so strong. The strength of the hand should approximate an opening bid, however.

You hold: (a) ♠A2 ♥43 ♦KQ765 ♣A1042
              (b) ♠A2 ♥43 ♦KQ1098 ♣A1042
              (c) ♠A2 ♥43 ♦KJ8762 ♣Q105
              (d) ♠A2 ♥43 ♦AJ10876 ♣Q105

East	South (you)
1♥	?

With (a), pass vulnerable, overcall 2♦ not vulnerable.
With (b), overcall 2♦ at any vulnerability.
With (c), pass vulnerable, overcall 2♦ not vulnerable.
With (d), overcall 2♦ at any vulnerability.

Beware of the death distribution: 5-3-3-2. With this distribution, the suit must be strong regardless of vulnerability.

104. Fourth seat action frequently depends upon the strength of your right hand opponent's response. If your right hand opponent has made a two over one response, beware! The opponents are in a power auction, and you should only bid with a strong suit to help direct a lead or suggest a sacrifice. Forget points. You are outgunned. The opponents figure to have at least 23 HCP between them, usually more.

You hold: (a) ♠KJ4 ♥AQ876 ♦A98 ♣J4
              (b) ♠5 ♥KQJ984 ♦Q1032 ♣32

West	North	East	South (you)
1♠	Pass	2♣	?

With (a), pass. Your suit is seedy, and you have losers from one end of your hand to another. Besides, partner figures to have two or three points at most.

With (b), bid 2♥. After a two-over-one start by the opponents, a fourth seat overcall should be thought of as a weak jump overcall.

32

105. Conversely, if responder makes a weak response, particularly a single raise, loosen up a bit. Two level overcalls can be made with 9-11 HCP and a reasonable suit. Jump overcalls are invitational, not weak.

You hold: ♠AKQ87 ♥43 ♦1076 ♣432

West	North	East	South (you)
1♥	Pass	2♥	?

Make the bid that hits you in the face, 2♠. If opener passes, partner can place the opponents with 18-21 HCP and will know your strength to within a point or two. Not to worry.

106. Jump overcalls of 2NT are unusual, showing 5-5 or 6-5 in the two lower ranking unbid suits. The range is usually 8-11 HCP.

(a) You hold: ♠4 ♥6 ♦A10876 ♣KJ8765

East	South(you)
1♥/♠	?

Overcall 2NT, and leave the rest to partner.

(b) You hold: ♠4 ♥KJ876 ♦AJ9876 ♣4

East	South (you)
1♣	?

Overcall 2NT, showing a red two-suiter (the two lower ranking unbid suits).

*107. A direct bid in the responder's suit is natural, typically showing a strong six card suit and 9-12 HCP. (Some play that it promises an opening bid.)

You hold: ♠4 ♥AK10976 ♦Q432 ♣86

West	North	East	South (you)
1♣	Pass	1♥	?

Bid 2♥. Don't wait around!

33

WHEN PARTNER OVERCALLS
- Tips 108 - 120

108. A single raise of an overcall is equal to the single raise of an opening bid - 7-10 support points. Give those raises!

109. With three card major suit support and a hand too strong for a single raise, cuebid.

You hold: (a) ♠A87 ♥54 ♦KQ87 ♣Q765
            (b) ♠A87 ♥54 ♦AK76 ♣Q765

West	North	East	South (you)
1♥	1♠	Pass	?

With both hands, bid 2♥.

110. With four card support and a hand too strong for a single raise, jump cuebid. The jump cuebid is invitational.

You hold: ♠KJ43 ♥87 ♦AQ98 ♣J43

West	North	East	South (you)
1♥	1♠	Pass	?

Bid 3♥. If partner rebids 3♠, you can pass if you like.

111. Jump raises of overcalls are preemptive (thus the need for the cuebids). Jump raises promise primary support, 3-6 HCP, and usually contain a singleton, particularly when vulnerable.

You hold: ♠A1043 ♥2 ♦J10543 ♣876

West	North	East	South (you)
1♥	1♠	2♥	?

Bid 3♠. Do not make the sissy bid of 2♠. There is no way you are going to buy this hand at 2♠. You might as well tell partner what you have. *This is an important tip.*

112. With three card major suit support, it is rare to change suits. A change of suit is not forcing and denies major suit support.

You hold: (a) ♠J104 ♥76 ♦AK1087 ♣987
           (b) ♠94 ♥42 ♦AKJ654 ♣943

West	North	East	South (you)
1♣	1♠	Pass	?

With (a), bid 2♠. A 2♦ bid would deny three spades.
With (b), bid 2♦, not forcing.

113. In response to a one level major suit overcall, a change of suit is not forcing and a jump in a new suit is invitational.

You hold: (a) ♠AK876 ♥2 ♦543 ♣K876
           (b) ♠AKJ104 ♥2 ♦A74 ♣Q1076

West	North	East	South (you)
1♦	1♥	Pass	?

With (a), bid 1♠, not forcing and denying opening bid values.
With (b), bid 2♠, invitational (12-15 HCP).

*114. In response to a *two-level* overcall, a change of suit is invitational; a jump in a new suit is forcing.

You hold: (a) ♠82 ♥AQJ94 ♦J732 ♣K3
           (b) ♠82 ♥AKJ974 ♦AQ5 94

West	North	East	South (you)
1♠	2♣	Pass	?

With (a), bid 2♥, invitational.
With (b), bid 3♥, forcing.

115. If partner's overcall is greeted with a negative double, make your normal raise with 7-10 HCP, cuebid with stronger raises, and redouble to show an opening bid lacking three card support.

You hold: (a) ♠Q87 ♥K87 ♦43 ♣Q10765
           (b) ♠AQ4 ♥K87 ♦43 ♣Q10876
           (c) ♠A1087 ♥J4 ♦432 ♣AKQ6

West	North	East	South (you)
1♦	1♥	Double	?

With (a), raise to 2♥.
With (b), cuebid 2♦.
With (c), redouble.

Note: Some play that the redouble simply shows the ace, king or
queen of partner's suit ... period.

116. When partner overcalls in a minor suit, with support set your
sights on 3NT. As ever, the cuebid is the stronger raise. The jump
cuebid is used to show support with a singleton in the opponents' suit.

You hold: (a) ♠87 ♥A873 ♦K876 ♣J43
           (b) ♠87 ♥AK87 ♦K876 ♣J43
           (c) ♠K87 ♥AQ4 ♦10652 ♣J43
           (d) ♠4 ♥A876 ♦K876 ♣AJ54

West	North	East	South (you)
1♠	2♣	Pass	?

With (a), raise to 3♣, the weakest raise, 7-9 support points.
With (b), cuebid 2♠, the stronger raise, 10+ support points.
With (c), bid 2NT. Even with support, notrump takes priority with a
stopper in the opponent's suit.
With (d), jump to 3♠ to show a strong hand in support of clubs with
a singleton spade, 13-16 support points.

117. Know your ranges when it comes to bidding notrump in response
to a one-level overcall. A 1NT response shows 8-11 HCP; a 2NT
response shows 12-14 HCP, and a 3NT response shows 15-18 HCP.
The 2NT response is not forcing.

You hold: (a) ♠75 ♥AQ4 ♦K1043 ♣J876
           (b) ♠82 ♥AQ4 ♦A954 ♣A1084
           (c) ♠J4 ♥AJ5 ♦KQJ9 ♣K1094

	West	North	East	South (you)
	1♣	1♠	Pass	?

With (a), bid 1NT.
With (b), bid 2NT.
With (c), bid 3NT.

118. After partner overcalls and you respond some number of no-trump, you promise one stopper, usually two, in the opponent's suit. You do not promise stoppers in the unbid suits, although it is a little easier on the nerves if you have them.

119. When considering a notrump response to a two level minor suit overcall, consider the degree of fit you have with partner's suit. If you have an honor in the suit, bid 2NT with 9-11 HCP, 3NT with more. If you don't have an honor, 10-12 is the range for a 2NT response.

You hold: (a) ♠AJ84 ♥J1043 ♦765 ♣K5
            (b) ♠AJ84 ♥J1043 ♦K543 ♣2

	West	North	East	South (you)
	1♠	2♣	Pass	?

With (a), bid 2NT. The ♣K is a big, big card.
With (b), pass. A singleton in partner's long suit should serve as a warning to bid conservatively. Reread this.

120. Holding strong primary trump support, make a jump raise regardless of how weak you are on the outside. Do not make a single raise! Reread this one. Again.

You hold: ♠AQ1043 ♥32 ♦432 ♣432

	West	North	East	South (you)
	1♥	1♠	P/2♣/♦/♥	?

Bid 3♠, preemptive, regardless of what East does.

This tip applies anytime you have strong trump support opposite a known two-suiter. Jump!

You hold: ♠432 ♥2 ♦AQ1065 ♣8765

North	East	South (you)	West
1♥	1♠	Pass	2♠
3♦	Pass	?	

Bid 5♦, not 4♦!

THE OVERCALLER'S REBID
- Tips 121 - 124

121. When partner changes suits, denying support for your suit, do not rebid your suit unless you have a strong six card suit.

You hold: (a) ♠AQ765 ♥876 ♦4 ♣A1086
            (b) ♠AQ10976 ♥876 ♦4 ♣A108

East	South	West	North
1♥	1♠	Pass	2♦
Pass	?		

With (a), pass. Partner doesn't have spades and you don't have diamonds. Get out while the getting is good. Partner's 2♦ bid is *not* forcing.
With (b), bid 2♠.

122. If partner bids notrump, bidding the opener's suit is natural and not forcing.

You hold: ♠5 ♥KQ876 ♦43 ♣KQJ76

East	South	West	North
1♣	1♥	Pass	1NT
Pass	?		

Bid 2♣ to show a heart-club two suiter.

123. After partner passes, bidding the opener's minor suit is natural and not forcing.

You hold: ♠3 ♥AK984 ♦KQJ104 ♣32

East	South (you)	West	North
1♦	1♥	Double*	Pass
1♠	?		

*Negative double

Bid 2♦. The level is cheap and your suit is good enough.

124. Be prepared for a cuebid. Assume partner has a strong raise (typically 11-13 support points), and wants to know more about your hand. If your rebid goes beyond the cheapest level of your suit, you promise an opening bid. A rebid of your original suit shows a minimum. A rebid in a lower ranking suit, forcing, does not promise an opening bid but may contain one. A return cue bid is a game force.

You hold: (a) ♠AQ1054 ♥87 ♦K54 ♣876
            (b) ♠AQ10543 ♥87 ♦K4 ♣K98
            (c) ♠AJ876 ♥KQ54 ♦65 ♣65
            (d) ♠AJ876 ♥KQ54 ♦A3 ♣65
            (e) ♠AJ943 ♥K4 ♦AJ5♣987
            (f) ♠AJ943 ♥1087 ♦AJ4 ♣108
            (g) ♠A10876 ♥3 ♦87 ♣KJ876
            (h) ♠A10876 ♥3 ♦87 ♣AK876
            (i) ♠AK8742 ♥2 ♦AQ94 ♣K3

East	South (you)	West	North
1♦	1♠	Pass	2♦
Pass	?		

With (a), bid 2♠, showing 8-11 HCP.

With (b), bid 3♠, invitational, 12-13 HCP.

With (c), bid 2♥, forcing but not necessarily promising a good hand. Pass if partner bids 2♠.

With (d), bid 2♥, but continue on over 2♠.

With (e), bid 2NT, invitational, showing 12-14 HCP with diamond strength.

With (f), bid 2♠ - not strong enough to bid 2NT.

With (g), bid 2♠ - not strong enough to bid 3♣.

With (h), bid 3♣.

With (i), bid 3♦, a game force. There might be a slam.

THE TAKEOUT DOUBLE: WHEN TO AND WHEN NOT TO - Tips 125-136

125. The ideal distribution for a takeout double is 4-4-4-1. Double with as few as 11 HCP if your right hand opponent opens in your short suit.

126. With 4-4-4-1 distribution and 11-17 HCP, pass if they open one of your four card suits. Later, if the opponents get together in your singleton suit, double for takeout.

You hold: ♠4 ♥AK76 ♦KJ76 ♣QJ87

East	South (you)
1♦	?

Pass. If West responds 1♠ and East raises, double for takeout.

127. Assume you hold 4-4 in the majors and 3-2 in the minors. With 12-15 HCP, double if your right hand opponent opens 1♣ or 1♦. Pass if your right hand opponent opens 1♥ or 1♠.

With 16-18 HCP, plus stoppers, double if your right hand opponent opens your short suit; otherwise, overcall 1NT. Overcall 1NT with 15 HCP plus two stoppers in their suit.

You hold: (a) ♠K1043 ♥AQ87 ♦543 ♣A2
(b) ♠AJ64 ♥QJ87 ♦AQ7 ♣K5
(c) ♠AK98 ♥AQ98 ♦AQ10 ♣54

East	South (you)
1♣/♦	?

With (a), double 1♣ or 1♦.
With (b), double 1♣; bid 1NT over 1♦.
With (c), double 1♣ or 1♦ — too strong to overcall 1NT over 1♦. (See tip #131.)

128. Assume you hold 4-4-3-2 distribution that does *not* include two four card majors, and the opponents open in one of your four card suits.

With 14 or fewer HCP, pass.
With exactly 15 HCP overcall 1NT if you have two stoppers in their suit; otherwise pass.
With 16-18 plus a stopper in their suit, overcall 1NT.
With 19 + HCP, double.

You hold: (a) ♠43 ♥KJ98 ♦AK75 ♣K102
           (b) ♠K4 ♥AQ87 ♦AJ76 ♣J104
           (c) ♠K4 ♥Q1042 ♦AJ5 ♣AKQJ

East	South (you)
1♥	?

With (a), pass.
With (b), overcall 1NT, 15 + HCP with two stoppers.
With (c), double.

129. It is risky to make a takeout double with a small doubleton in an unbid major. In order to pull this one off, you should have 19 + HCP.

You hold: (a) ♠87 ♥AQ87 ♦AKJ7 ♣AJ7
           (b) ♠87 ♥AQ76 ♦AJ87 ♣AJ9

East	South (you)
1♣	?

With (a), double. If partner bids 1♠, rebid 1NT, showing 18-19 HCP.
With (b), overcall 1NT directly. You are not strong enough to double and then bid 1NT over the expected spade response.

130. With five-three distribution in the majors and four-one in the minors, overcall a major suit at the one level with 8-15 HCP, regardless of which suit is opened to your right.

With 15-16 or more HCP, double if they open the singleton; overcall if they do not.

With exactly 15 HCP, you must make a battlefield decision.

42

You hold: (a) ♠A92 ♥KQ765 ♦4 ♣AJ43
         (b) ♠K92 ♥AK1087 ♦4 ♣AJ103
         (c) ♠QJ4 ♥KQ873 ♦4 ♣AK87
         (d) ♠A93 ♥KQ873 ♦4 ♣AK87

East	South (you)
1♦	?

With (a), bid 1♥ - not strong enough to double and then bid hearts.
With (b), double - superior 15 count.
With (c), Bid 1♥ - an average 15 count.
With (d), double - strong enough to double and then bid hearts.

131. A takeout double followed by a 1NT rebid is stronger than overcalling 1NT directly.

(a)
East	South	West	North
1♣	Double	Pass	1♦
Pass	1NT		

(b)
East	South
1♣	1NT

In (a), South has 18-19 HCP.
In (b), South has 16-18 HCP. (Some 18 point hands are better than others.)

132. A takeout double followed by a suit rebid is stronger than overcalling the suit directly.

(a)
East	South	West	North
1♦	Double	Pass	1♥
Pass	1♠		

(b)
East	South	West	North
1♦	1♠		

In (a), South generally has either 17-18 HCP with 5-3-3-2 distribution or 16-18 HCP with 5-4-3-1 distribution. Exceptionally, South will have a six card suit.
In (b), South has a range of 8-16 HCP!

133. After you make an overcall, you can still make a takeout double - providing the opponents find a fit and partner has not bid.

You hold: ♠AK876 ♥32 ♦AJ4 ♣K65

East	South (you)	West	North
1♥	1♠	2♥	Pass
Pass	?		

Double — Not strong enough to double and then bid spades (17 + HCP), but strong enough to bid spades and then double. This sequence shows 13-16 HCP, shortness in the opponents' suit, and at least three cards in each of the unbid suits.

134. With eight or nine winners in your own hand plus a stopper in the opener's suit, overcall 3NT. Don't worry about points; this bid shows tricks!

You hold: ♠K ♥K4 ♦AKQ10976 ♣A43

East	South (you)
1♥	?

Are you a man or a mouse? Overcall 3NT. Hide your ♠K in with your clubs if it will make you feel any better.

135. With eight or nine winners in your own hand but no stopper in the *major* suit opened to your right, make a jump cuebid! (A new toy!) It asks partner to bid 3NT with a stopper in the opener's suit.

You hold: ♠A4 ♥76 ♦K4 ♣AKQJ876

East	South (you)
1♥	?

Overcall 3♥. With a heart stopper, partner bids 3NT. If you do not hear 3NT, bid clubs .

136. A direct jump bid in the opponent's *minor* suit is natural, showing a seven card suit with less than opening bid values.

You hold: ♠A4 ♥5 ♦876 ♣KQ109765

East	South (you)
1♣	?

Bid 3♣ and let the opponents sort out what to do. They may not know that a double by the responder in this sequence is for takeout. Shh, don't tell them.

RESPONDING TO A TAKEOUT DOUBLE
- Tips 137 - 151

137. When considering a suit response, do not count points for jacks and queens in the opponents' suit.

138. Add one point for any five card suit and three points for any six card suit.

139. When responding in a suit, make a non-jump response with 0-8, a jump response with 9-11, and cuebid or bid game with 12 +.

You hold: (a) ♠AJ765 ♥543 ♦K4 ♣876
            (b) ♠AK65 ♥543 ♦K42 ♣876
            (c) ♠32 ♥543 ♦65 ♣AK10876
            (d) ♠AJ765 ♥Q54 ♦Q32 ♣54
            (e) ♠A87 ♥32 ♦AJ87 ♣K542

West	North	East	South (you)
1♥	Double	Pass	?

With (a), bid 2♠. Counting one extra point for your five card suit, you have 9 points. This jump is *not forcing*.
With (b), bid 2♠. You are allowed to jump on a four card suit.
With (c), bid 3♣. This hand is worth 10 points after adding three for your six card suit.
With (d), Bid 1♠. Do not count for the ♥Q. If the ♥Q were the ♣Q, bid 2♠.
With (e), bid 2♥ - Too strong to make a jump response.

140. With a four card major and a five card minor, plus a hand too weak to jump or cuebid, answer in the major.

You hold: ♠K1043 ♥54 ♦Q7654 ♣32

West	North	East	South (you)
1♥	Double	Pass	?

Respond 1♠.

46

141. With a four card major and a six card minor, plus a hand too weak to jump or cuebid, answer in the minor.

You hold: ♠K1043 ♥43 ♦Q87654 ♣5

West	North	East	South (you)
1♥	Double	Pass	?

Respond 2♦. You will bid spades later.

142. A 1NT response shows 7-9 HCP, a 2NT response 10-12 HCP, and a 3NT response 13-16 HCP. However, in response to a double of 1♥ or 1♠, a 1NT response can be shaded to 5-6 HCP. These responses promise at least one stopper in the opponent's suit, frequently two.

You hold: (a) ♠KQJ4 ♥876 ♦943 ♣765
        (b) ♠K1032 ♥653 ♦87 ♣8765
        (c) ♠AQ4 ♥K54 ♦J87 ♣K1065
        (d) ♠AQ32 ♥K4 ♦Q1043 ♣432

West	North	East	South (you)
1♠	Double	Pass	?

With (a), bid 1NT.
With (b), bid 2♣. You can only shade a 1NT response so much.
With (c), bid 3NT.
With (d), bid 2NT.

143. You do not need stoppers in unbid suits to bid notrump. What you do need is at least one stopper, preferably two, in the opponents' suit.

144. When faced with a choice of either cuebidding or jumping in notrump, strength in the opponent's suit is the deciding factor. The more strength, the more likely the notrump response.

You hold: (a) ♠AQJ ♥10876 ♦KJ4 ♣J54
        (b) ♠A87 ♥A987 ♦Q1043 ♣Q5

West	North	East	South (you)
1♠	Double	Pass	?

With (a), bid 2NT.
With (b), start with 2♠.

145. A cuebid followed by a new suit is forcing.

You hold: ♠7 ♥A76 ♦J98 ♣AQ10765

West	North	East	South (you)
1♥	Double	Pass	?

Bid 2♥ and then bid clubs later to create a force. Do not make the lazy response of 3♣ which is *not* forcing.

146. There is one case where you are allowed to cuebid with fewer than 12 points. When you have four cards in both unbid majors and 9 + HCP, you are allowed to cuebid. A cuebid followed by a raise is *not* forcing.

You hold: (a) ♠AJ54 ♥KJ98 ♦432 ♣54
          (b) ♠AJ54 ♥KJ98 ♦432 ♣K4

West	North	East	South (you)
1♦	Double	Pass	?

With (a), bid 2♦ and raise partner's likely major suit rebid to the three level, not forcing.
With (b), bid 2♦ and jump raise partner's likely major suit rebid to game.

147. After you have made a minimum response showing 0-8 to a takeout double, you are allowed to bid again opposite a silent partner. However, to do so, you should have 6-8 points and either a five card suit, a strong four carder or a second suit.

You hold: ♠KQ104 ♥765 ♦J1032 ♣87

West	North	East	South (you)
1♥	Double	Pass	1♠
2♥	Pass	Pass	?

Bid 2♠. Partner must have spade support for the takeout double.

148. When your right hand opponent bids, you are off the hook. Nevertheless, make an effort to squeak, if possible. A one level squeak shows 5-8 points, a two level squeak 6-9, and to come in at the three level requires 8-10. With stronger hands, jump or cuebid.

You hold: ♠KJ98 ♥876 ♦Q107 ♣432

West	North	East	South (you)
1♥	Double	2♥/3♥	?

Over 2♥, bid 2♠. Over 3♥, pass.

149. There are times when you must respond on a three card suit. When this happens, respond in the cheaper or cheapest three card suit, not the strongest.

You hold: ♠Q98 ♥1087 ♦87654 ♣J2

West	North	East	South (you)
1♦	Double	Pass	?

You must bid something. Your diamonds are not nearly strong enough to consider a penalty pass. A 1NT response to a minor suit takeout double shows 7-9 HCP. You have no alternative but to bid 1♥, — audibly, please.

*150. A *jump* cuebid shows a solid minor suit and asks partner to bid notrump with a stopper in the opponent's suit.

You hold: ♠76 ♥87 ♦543 ♣AKQJ98

West	North	East	South (you)
1♥	Double	Pass	?

Bid 3♥. If partner has read this book, the meaning will be clear. If he hasn't, why hasn't he?

151. Do not pass a low level takeout double because of weakness. The only excuse for passing is length and strength in the opponent's suit: either five cards headed by three of the top five honors or six cards headed by two or three of the top five honors. With only five cards,

the intermediates must also be exceptional. If they are not, find some bid.

You hold: (a) ♠4 ♥AJ10843 ♦43 ♣J876
              (b) ♠43 ♥KQJ98 ♦43 ♣Q876
              (c) ♠43 ♥KQ654 ♦432 ♣Q76

West	North	East	South (you)
1♥	Double	Pass	?

With (a), pass.
With (b), pass - good intermediates.
With (c), bid 1NT - poor intermediates.

THE REBID BY THE TAKEOUT DOUBLER
- Tips 152 - 160

152. Once you make a takeout double with minimum values, do not bid again unless partner makes a forcing bid or bids two suits requesting a preference.

You hold: ♠A1054 ♥KJ4 ♦54 ♣AJ32

East	South (you)	West	North
1♦	Double	Pass	2♥
Pass	?		

Pass. 2♥ is not forcing. Partner may have four hearts.

153. A raise of a forced response shows 16-18 support points and guarantees primary support (four or more cards). In competition, the raise can be made with 15 support points but still guarantees primary support.

You hold: ♠AK87 ♥K94 ♦43 ♣KJ76

(a)
East	South (you)	West	North
1♦	Double	Pass	1♠
Pass	?		

(b)
East	South (you)	West	North
1♦	Double	Pass	1♠
2♦	?		

With (a), pass.
With (b), compete to 2♠.

If partner responds 1♥, pass with both hands.

154. A jump raise shows 19-21 support points along with primary support.

You hold: ♠AK87 ♥2 ♦AQ8 ♣K10985

East	South (you)	West	North
1♥	Double	Pass	1♠
Pass	?		

Jump to 3♠, highly invitational.

155. After a forced response, a jump shift is invitational (19-20 HCP). To force, cuebid and then bid a suit.

You hold: (a) ♠AQ1065 ♥KQ4 ♦4 ♣AKJ8
(b) ♠AQ1064 ♥AK4 ♦4 ♣AKJ8

East	South (you)	West	North
1♦	Double	Pass	1♥
Pass	?		

With (a), bid 2♠, highly invitational.
With (b), bid 2♦, and then bid spades to create a force.

156. After a forced response, a new suit shows 16-18 HCP and is invitational.

You hold: ♠AJ4 ♥AK876 ♦4 ♣A1095

East	South (you)	West	North
1♦	Double	Pass	1♠
Pass	?		

Bid 2♥, mildly invitational. The 2♥ bid shows a five card suit. Partner is supposed to rebid spades holding five spades and one or two hearts.

157. After any jump response, including 2NT, a new suit is forcing.

(a)
East	South (you)	West	North
1♦	Double	Pass	2♥
Pass	2♠	Pass	?

(b)
East	South (you)	West	North
1♦	Double	Pass	2NT
Pass	3♥	Pass	?

In both cases, South's last bid is forcing.

158. If partner responds at the two level in competition, a new suit is invitational. If partner responds at the three level in competition, a new suit is forcing.

(a) East	South	West	North
1♦	Double	2♦	2♥
Pass	2♠	Pass	?

(b) East	South	West	North
1♦	Double	2♦	3♣
Pass	3♠	Pass	?

In (a), the 2♠ rebid is invitational.
In (b), the 3♠ rebid is forcing.

159. After a 1NT response, a new suit is not forcing, a jump is invitational. To force, cuebid and then bid a suit.

You hold: (a) ♠A1054 ♥K876 ♦KJ1054 ♣-
           (b) ♠AJ72 ♥A43 ♦KQJ432 ♣-
           (c) ♠KQ7 ♥AQ9742 ♦A106 ♣A

East	South (you)	West	North
1♣	Double	Pass	1NT
Pass	?		

With (a), bid 2♦, not forcing.
With (b), bid 3♦, invitational.
With (c), bid 2♣ and then bid hearts to create a force.

160. Doubling the same suit twice, or even three times, does not alter the original meaning of the double - takeout. However, if the second or third double comes at the game level, partner only removes with an unbalanced hand.

You hold: ♠AQ87 ♥5 ♦AQ87 ♣AKJ4

East	South (you)	West	North
1♥	Double	2♥	Pass
Pass	Double	3♥	Pass
Pass	?		

Double again. Even though you sound like a broken record, each successive double shows more and more strength. A third double shows 18-20 HCP minimum.

OPENER'S REVERSE - Tips 161 - 169

161. Whenever opener bids two suits, forcing a *three* level preference to the first suit, opener has reversed.

(a) **Opener**	**Responder**	(b) **Opener**	**Responder**
1♥	1♠	1♦	1♠
2♦		2♥	

In (a), opener has not reversed.
In (b), opener has reversed, by forcing a three level preference.

162. A reverse after a one level response is a one round force. A reverse after a two level response is a game force.

163. Most reverses show five cards in the first suit, four in the second. Some reverses show six cards in the first suit and four in the seond. Reverses with 4-4 distribution are rare.

164. After a one level response, opener's reverse shows 17 + HCP with 5-4 distribution. With 6-4, the minimum is 15 HCP — providing the hand either has concentrated strength in the two suits or the six card suit has good intermediates. If it doesn't, rebid the six card suit.

You hold: (a) ♠Q2 ♥AK87 ♦AJ1043 ♣32
           (b) ♠54 ♥AK87 ♦AKQJ2 ♣43
           (c) ♠2 ♥AK87 ♦AKJ876 ♣32
           (d) ♠2 ♥KQ87 ♦AJ7654 ♣KQ

South (you)	**North**
1♦	1♠
?	

With (a), rebid 2♦ - not strong enough to rebid 2♥ and force a three level preference. A 1NT rebid hints at a common disease, "notrump-itis."

With (b), rebid 2♥. This hand is better than it looks because it has concentrated strength.

With (c), rebid 2♥. Once again, concentrated strength.

With (d), rebid 2♦ - Diamonds not strong enough, not to mention the flaw in clubs.

*165. After a *two* level response, a reverse can be made with as few as 15 HCP.

You hold: (a) ♠42 ♥KQ87 ♦AKJ54 ♣43
         (b) ♠42 ♥KQ87 ♦AQ1087 ♣A3

South (you)	West	North	East
1♦	Pass	1♠	Pass
?			

With (a), rebid 2♦.
With (b), rebid 2♥.

166. Do not "invent" a reverse with 5-5 distribution. Open the bidding in the higher ranking suit.

You hold: ♠3 ♥AKJ76 ♦AKJ87 ♣Q3

Open 1♥. To open this hand 1♦ is a colossal bridge blunder. Actually, it's worse.

167. A jump reverse carries a special meaning and will be discussed in the chapter on Splinter Jumps.

168. In competition, a reverse may not always be a reverse.

(a) South (you)	West	North	East
1♦	2♣	2♥	Pass
2♠			

(b) South (you)	West	North	East
1♥	2♣	2♦	Pass
2♠			

In (a), partner's response at the two level *outranked* your first suit, making it impossible to rebid your original suit at the two level. When that happens, mentioning a higher ranking suit is not considered a reverse. It can be made with a minimum opening bid.

In (b), partner's two level response was in a *lower* ranking suit. Had you wished, you could have rebid your original suit with a minimum. In (b), you have reversed.

56

169. The "big boys" sometimes manufacture a reverse on a three card suit with 6-3-3-1 distribution in order to create a force.

You hold: ♠AQ4 ♥KQ4 ♦5 ♣AK8765

South (you)	North
1♣	1♠
?	

Your best rebid is 2♥! Any jump in spades promises primary support; a jump in clubs is not forcing and you could lose a spade contract.

2♥, forcing, gives you a chance to support spades later and show three card support. In addition, if partner raises hearts showing primary support, partner must have five spades! With four hearts and four spades, partner responds 1♥.

WHEN PARTNER REVERSES
- Tips 170-176

170. Do not pass. Life is too short; besides, the bid is forcing.

171. With 8+ HCP, insist upon game; with an opening bid, think about slam; with an opening bid plus, get your side to slam unless the hand is misfitted.

*172. You must have some way to sign off after a reverse with hands in the 5-7 HCP range. There are two ways: (1) rebid your suit, forcing, but you can then pass partner's next bid if you wish; or (2) rebid 2NT, forcing partner to rebid his original suit (unless he has extras). After that rebid, you can either pass or make a non- forcing rebid of your own.

You hold: (a) ♠KQ874 ♥432 ♦876 ♣J4
           (b) ♠KQ87 ♥432 ♦J1042 ♣76

North	South(you)
1♣	1♠
2♦	?

With (a), rebid 2♠ and pass partner's next bid if it is not forcing. A new suit by partner would be forcing.
With (b), rebid 2NT and correct partner's forced 3♣ rebid to 3♦, not forcing. A direct raise to 3♦ would be a game force.

173. After a reverse, if you do not rebid your original suit or rebid 2NT, artificial, the partnership is in a game- forcing auction.

174. If you have an overwhelming desire to bid notrump, with 8-9 HCP, bid 2NT and then 3NT. With 10-12 HCP bid 3NT directly. With 13-14, bid 2NT and then 4NT, natural.

You hold: (a) ♠KQ87 ♥K108 ♦432 ♣654
             (b) ♠KQ87 ♥KQ9 ♦432 ♣765
             (c) ♠K9876 ♥KJ8 ♦KQJ ♣32

North	South (you)
1♣	1♠
2♦	?

With (a), bid 2NT and then 3NT.
With (b), bid 3NT.
With (c), bid 2NT and then 4NT.

175. A jump raise of the second suit shows good trumps. It is a *mild* slam try.

You hold: (a) ♠A8765 ♥KQ98 ♦43 ♣32
             (b) ♠A8765 ♥Q543 ♦43 ♣K2

North	East	South (you)	West
1♦	Pass	1♠	Pass
2♥	Pass	?	

With (a), bid 4♥ to emphasize the trump strength.
With (b), bid 3♥, a game force. Hearts not strong enough to jump.

176. A return to partner's first suit is a forward going bid. It is a game force. (See tip #173.)

You hold: ♠AJ742 ♥J4 ♦A106 ♣876

North	South (you)
1♦	1♠
2♥	?

Bid 3♦, forward going. No, don't tell me you wanted to rebid those spades. Just don't tell me that.

SPLINTER JUMPS BY THE OPENER
- Tips 177-195

177. A jump rebid by the opener one level higher than a jump shift is called a "splinter jump."

(a) South	North	(b) South	North	(c) South	North
1♥	1♠	1♥	1♠	1♥	1♠
2♣		3♣		4♣	

In (a), 2♣ is a natural rebid, normally showing five hearts and four clubs.

In (b), 3♣ is a jump shift, forcing to game. It neither promises nor denies spade support.

In (c), opener has made a splinter jump. A splinter jump *promises* primary support for responder's suit, a singleton in the jump suit and 18-20 support points.

Opener may hold: ♠KQ76 ♥AK1043 ♦K105 ♣3

178. As the key to most successful slams is having the "right" singleton, splinter jumps are invaluable.

Opener	Responder	Opener	Responder
♠4	♠8732	1♦	1♥
♥A1087	♥KQ9432	3♠	4NT
♦AQJ87	♦2	5♠	6♥
♣AJ3	♣K4	Pass	

The key bid in the sequence is opener's splinter jump to 3♠. Responder's hand has become enormous opposite spade shortness, and an easy slam is reached.

179. After a one level response, a jump reverse is a splinter.

You hold: (a) ♠2 ♥AKJ4 ♦AKJ87 ♣K32
(b) ♠AQ74 ♥3 ♦AK754 ♣KJ4

South (you)	North
1♦	1♠
?	

60

With (a), bid 2♥; a reverse is a one round force.
With (b), bid 3♥, a jump reverse. A jump reverse is both a splinter and a game force.

180. After a *two* level response, a jump reverse is a splinter.

You hold: ♠4 ♥AK4 ♦AJ876 ♣KJ43

South (you)	North
1♦	2♣
?	

Bid 3♠, a jump reverse (splinter).

*181. After a *two* level response, a jump shift is a splinter.

You hold: (a) ♠AKJ87 ♥AK1054 ♦KJ ♣3
 (b) ♠AKJ87 ♥2 ♦KJ87 ♣K98

South (you)	North
1♠	2♦
?	

With (a), bid 2♥, forcing.
With (b), bid 3♥, a splinter.

Many players use the jump shift to 3♥ as a natural bid showing a strong 5-5 hand. Those players bid 3♥ with (a) and 3♦ or 4♦ with (b).

182. If you agree with the two previous tips , all second round jumps by the opener after a *two* level response are splinters.

183. If the opponents overcall, you can only splinter in their suit(s). In the long run, this tip will save you *mucho* grief. Experts, of course, make exceptions.

South (you)	West	North	East
1♦	1♥	?	

North-South can only splinter in hearts. However, if East bids clubs, North-South can also splinter in that suit.

You hold: (a) ♠AQ42 ♥3 ♦KQ876 ♣AJ5
(b) ♠AQ42 ♥AJ5 ♦KQ876 ♣3

South (you)	West	North	East
1♦	1♥	1♠	2♣
?			

With (a), jump to 3♥.
With (b), jump to 4♣.

*184. A jump rebid one level higher than a splinter jump shows a void in the jump suit.

You hold: (a) ♠4 ♥AQ87 ♦KQ876 ♣AK4
(b) ♠AQ87 ♥4 ♦KJ1054 ♣AK6
(c) ♠KQ87 ♥ − ♦AK8765 ♣K98

South (you)	North
1♦	1♠
?	

With (a), bid 2♥, forcing.
With (b), splinter to 3♥, a game force, showing a singleton heart.
With (c), splinter to 4♥, showing a heart void.

Some players use 3♥ and 4♥ to describe splinters of varying strength and make no distinction between singletons and voids.

185. After partner has made an unlimited response, a splinter jump is a game force. After partner has made a limited response, a splinter jump is a slam try. See the following tip.

186. Opener can splinter after responder rebids a suit. These splinters are slam tries because responder is *limited*.

You hold: ♠K76 ♥2 ♦AKQ104 ♣AJ87

South (you)	North
1♦	1♠
2♣	2♠
?	

Bid 4 ♥, a splinter jump. After partner has rebid a suit, splinter jumps show three card support. Otherwise, primary support is guaranteed! Reread this.

187. Splinter jumps are not toys. Unless both you and your partner are sure you can recognize one of these "crazy" leaps, better to forget about them. These is no bridge disaster quite like a splinter disaster!

188. A first round jump by the responder one level higher than a jump shift is a splinter.

You hold: ♠A87 ♥KJ876 ♦3 ♣K1054

North	South (you)
1♥	?

Bid 4 ♦, one level higher than a jump shift to show the singleton with a game forcing hand (12-15 support points).

*189. Although many play some form of splinter in response to a major suit opening, not everyone does so in response to a minor suit opening. The tip from here is to play them in both instances.

You hold: (a) ♠3 ♥A87 ♦KQ8765 ♣Q109
(b) ♠KJ109874 ♥4 ♦Q32 ♣87

North	South (you)
1♦	?

With (a), you are thrilled that you can respond 3♠ to show this hand type.
With (b), you are annoyed that you cannot bid 3♠ to show a preemptive type hand. Whenever you play a convention, you have to give up something. If you play that 3♠ is a splinter, then you must respond 1♠ with (b). Not playing splinters, you have a difficult responding problem with (a).

190. A splinter response to a minor suit opening bid denies a four card major.

You hold: ♠KJ87 ♥4 ♦AJ1065 ♣K43

63

North   South (you)
　1♦　　　　?

Respond 1♠. Do not splinter in hearts with an unbid four card major.

191. After opener rebids the first suit, responder can make a second round splinter jump with three card support.

You hold: ♠A43 ♥5 ♦KQ987 ♣AQ43

North   South (you)
　1♠　　　2♦
　2♠　　　?

Jump to 4♥ to show slam interest, three card support and a singleton heart. You can't do much better than that. Rebidding 3♣ and then supporting spades *denies* a singleton heart; for example, you might have: ♠43 ♥54 ♦KQ987 ♣AQ4.

192. After opener rebids a major suit at the one level, jumps to the *four* level are splinter jumps.

You hold: ♠KJ87 ♥AQJ65 ♦4 ♣K54

North   South (you)
　1♣　　　1♥
　1♠　　　?

Jump to 4♦ to show the singleton diamond. A jump to 3♦ is natural. A jump to 4♣, partner's suit, is considered a splinter, as well.

193. When the opponents overcall, a jump in their suit is a game forcing splinter, showing a singleton. A jump one level higher shows a void.

You hold:　(a) ♠A87 ♥3 ♦J1054 ♣AK987
　　　　　　(b) ♠A87 ♥- ♦J1054 ♣AK9876

North   East   South   West
　1♣　　　1♥　　　?

With (a), bid 3♥.
With (b), bid 4♥. You're in the fast lane now!

*194. When a splinter jump is doubled, a return to the trump suit is the weakest possible bid. A pass indicates further slam interest.

You hold: (a) ♠KJ543 ♥KJ4 ♦43 ♣876
 (b) ♠KQ543 ♥876 ♦QJ10 ♣Q10

North	East	South (you)	West
1♣	Pass	1♠	Pass
3♥	Double	?	

With (a), return to 3♠; you have wasted heart strength.
With (b), pass. You still have slam interest, but nothing to cuebid.

195. When a splinter jump is doubled, "redouble" shows the ace of the splinter suit.

You hold: ♠KJ1087 ♥A876 ♦J4 ♣108

North	East	South (you)	West
1♦	Pass	1♠	Pass
3♥	Double	?	

Redouble to show the ♥A.

BELOVED BLACKWOOD - Tips 196-200

196. Every 4NT bid is *not* Blackwood, and "premature" Blackwood is not the best way to get to or stay out of many slams.

197. In most slam auctions, the stronger hand bids Blackwood. The weak hand tells; the strong hand asks. Reread this one.

198. Do not use Blackwood prematurely when you have two or more losers in an unbid suit.

You hold: ♠KQ987 ♥Q107 ♦AKJ7 ♣2

North	South (you)
1♣	1♠
3♠	?

Cuebid 4♦. Do not bid 4NT ... yet. You have two quick losers in hearts. You need some sort of heart cuebid from partner.

199. Do not use Blackwood prematurely with a void.

You hold: ♠AKQ876 ♥- ♦KQ8 ♣AKQ3

South (you)	North
2♣*	2♦
2♠	3♠
?	

*Strong and artificial.

Cuebid 4♣, hoping for a 4♦ cuebid from partner. Rushing the net with a premature 4NT bid is about the worst thing you can do. Say partner does have one ace. How does that help when you don't know which one it is?

*200. Do not ask partner for kings unless you have all four aces between the two hands. Partner is allowed to jump to seven in response to 5NT!

You hold: ♠KQ10876 ♥2 ♦AQJ4 ♣K4

North	South (you)
1♥	1♠
3♠	4NT
5♥	?

Bid 6♠. Do not bid 5NT asking for kings. You are missing an ace.

At matchpoints, this rule is often waived in order to be able to play the hand in 6NT.

WHEN PARTNER BIDS
BELOVED BLACKWOOD - Tips 201-210

201. Respond 5♣ with either no aces or all four aces. If partner can't tell the difference from your previous bidding, either you can't bid or partner can't play.

202. Do not count a void as an ace.

203. With one or three aces, plus a working void (not a void in partner's first bid suit), jump to six of the void suit if the void suit is *lower* ranking than the trump suit. If the void suit is *higher* ranking than the trump suit, jump to six of the trump suit.

You hold: (a) ♠ — ♥AJ432 ♦J10876 ♣J87
          (b) ♠J10876 ♥AJ432 ♦J87 ♣ —

North	South (you)
1♥	4♥
4NT	?

With (a), respond 6♥ to show one (or three aces) plus a *higher* ranking void. (Do you think partner can work out where your void is?)

With (b), respond 6♣ to show one ace (or three) with a club void.

As ever, your previous bidding determines whether you have one or three aces. As the stronger hand usually bids Blackwood, nine times out of ten, the jump response shows one ace.

204. With zero or two aces, plus a working void, respond 5NT.

You hold: ♠876 ♥AJ10876 ♦ — ♣AJ32

North	South (you)
1♠	2♥
4NT	?

Respond 5NT to show two aces plus a void which can't be in spades.

205. If partner cuebids your void suit and then bids 4NT, disregard the void and answer aces.

You hold: ♠1094 ♥ — ♦A8765 ♣J10876

North	East	South (you)	West
1♠	2♥	2♠	3♥
4♥	Pass	4♠	Pass
4NT	Pass	?	

Respond 5♦. Disregard the heart void. Partner has cuebid the suit.

206. If the opponents mess with (interfere) partner's Blackwood bid *beneath* the five level of your agreed suit, double with no aces, pass with one ace, and bid the next ranking suit with two aces, etc. This is called "DOPI" (like the dwarf). "D" stands for double; "O" stands for zero; "P" stands for pass; and "I" stands for one.

You hold: ♠A876 ♥87 ♦KJ104 ♣Q54

North	East	South	West
1♠	Pass	3♠	4♥
4NT	5♥	?	

Pass to show one ace.

207. If the opponents interfere with partner's Blackwood bid *above* the five level of your agreed suit, double with an even number of aces; pass with an odd number. Do not bid on.

This convention is called "DEPO" (pronounced depot). The "D" stands for double; the "E" stands for even; the "P" stands for pass; and "O" stands for odd.

You hold: (a) ♠KJ87 ♥87 ♦KQ104 ♣J54
         (b) ♠A876 ♥87 ♦KQ104 ♣J54

South (you)	West	North	East
Pass	Pass	1♠	4♥
4♠	Pass	4NT	6♣
?			

With (a), double to show an even number of aces.
With (b), pass to show an odd number of aces.

208. If you can count 13 tricks, do not answer for kings. Bid 7!

You hold: ♠6 ♥KQ1076543 ♦KQ4 ♣4

South (you)	West	North	East
4♥	4♠	4NT	Pass
5♣	Pass	5NT	Pass
?			

Partner must have all four aces to bid 5NT. Bid seven. (See next tip.)

209. When you can count 13 top tricks, bid 7NT, regardless of how good a fit you may have. In a suit contract, you run the risk of the opening lead being ruffed. In the previous example, bid 7NT, not 7♥.

210. If clubs or diamonds is the agreed suit and partner bids 4NT and then 5♠ over your response, bid 5NT. Don't worry, just do it! The hand is missing two aces and partner wants to get out at 5NT.

You hold: ♠87 ♥KQ765 ♦4 ♣AJ1073

North	South (you)
1♣	1♥
2♦	4♣
4NT	5♦
5♠	?

Bid 5NT. It is not for you to reason why; it is for you to do or die!

MORE SLAM BIDDING AIDS
- Tips 211-227

211. A raise or jump to the *five* level of the *agreed* major asks you to bid slam with first or second round control in the *unbid* suit.

You hold: ♠QJ4 ♥J765 ♦AKJ8 ♣Q4

South (you)	North
1♦	2♥
3♥	4♣
4♦	5♥
?	

Partner's leap asks about spades. You have neither first nor second round control. Pass.

212. If the opponents have bid one suit, a raise or leap to the five level of the agreed major asks you to bid a slam with first or second round control in their suit.

You hold: ♠87 ♥KJ8765 ♦ — ♣AKJ94

South (you)	West	North	East
1♥	3♠	5♥	Pass
?			

Pass. You have neither first nor second round control in their suit.

213. Do not confuse the raise to the five level of the agreed suit with a competitive bid at the five level.

(a) South	West	North	East
1♥	4♠	5♥	Pass
?			

(b) South	West	North	East
1♥	2♠	3♦	3♠
4♥	Pass	5♥	Pass
?			

71

In (a), 5♥ is competitive and does not ask about spades.
In (b), 5♥ is not competitive because your right hand opponent has passed. 5♥ asks about spades. The key is whether the non-jump raise comes after a pass or after a bid. After a pass, it asks; after a bid, it does not.

214. When answering a five level asking bid, pass, lacking first or second round control in the ask suit; bid 5NT with the guarded king; bid six of the agreed suit with a singleton; cuebid their suit with the ace. A grand slam may be in the offing!

Opener (you)	Responder
♠5	♠1087
♥QJ876	♥AK1032
♦AKQ4	♦—
♣543	♣AKQ76

South	West	North	East
1♥	3♠	5♥	Pass
?			

Bid 6♥; you have a singleton spade. With the ♠A, bid 5♠.

215. After partner makes a limit raise, do not even think about a slam unless you have a singleton or void.

You hold: ♠AQ3 ♥KQ5 ♦K4 ♣AJ876

North	South (you)
Pass	1♣
3♣	?

No singleton; no void; no slam! Bid 3NT.

216. Do not refuse a slam try when you have *unexpectedly* good trumps, regardless of outside strength (or lack of it). Jump in the trump suit.

You hold: ♠76 ♥AKQ76 ♦8765 ♣32

North	South (you)
1♥	3♥ (limit raise)
3♠	?

72

Bid 5♥. Partner is making a slam try with a terrible trump suit. Your jump shows great trumps, nothing else.

217. If notrump has not been bid previously, a *leap* to 5NT, the Grand Slam Force, asks a specific question: Which honors do you have in the agreed suit? If there is no agreed suit, which honors do you have in the last bid suit?

(a) North	South	(b) North	South
1♥	5NT	1♣	1♠
?		3♠	5NT
		?	

In (a), South asks about honors in hearts, the last bid suit.
In (b), South asks about honors in spades, the agreed suit.

*218. When responding to the Grand Slam force, respond:

6♣ - With the queen or less. If the queen is needed for seven, partner bids 6♦.
6♦ - With the ace or king and minimum length for your previous bidding.
6♥ - With the ace or king and maximum length for your previous bidding.
7♣ - With two of the top three honors. Partner will convert to seven of the agreed suit.

219. In order to use the Grand Slam Force, you must be sure there are no losers in the side suits and you must have one of the top three honors in the trump suit.

Opener	Responder		Opener	Responder
♠A98765	♠KJ32		1♠	5NT
♥QJ4	♥A2		6♥	7♠
♦2	♦AK87654		Pass	
♣KQ8	♣ —			

Responder hauls out the trusty Grand Slam Force and opener shows the ♠A or ♠K with extra length. Normal length would be five cards, so responder assumes six. Knowing of a ten card spade fit, responder can bid the Grand Slam even though the opponents have the ♠Q.

*220. When *clubs* is the agreed suit, 4NT is a risky ace ask. The response might easily push you beyond the safety level of 5♣. A better idea is to use a jump to the four level of the cheapest unbid suit to ask for aces after clubs have been agreed at the three level.

Opener	Responder		Opener	Responder
♠AK1043	♠J		1♣	1♥
♥4	♥KQ876		1♠	3♣
♦3	♦J107		4♦	4♠
♣KQ10876	♣AJ94		5♣	Pass

What does it all mean? Responder gives a non-forcing jump preference to 3♣, and opener wishes to ask for aces. Rather than jump to 4NT, opener, by agreement, jumps to the cheapest unbid suit at the four level to ask for aces. Responder shows one ace, and opener settles in the comfortable contract of 5♣. Contrast this with the opener leaping to 4NT and hearing a 5♦ response. Help! This little gem of an idea goes under the title of "Super Gerber." Super Gerber, like splinter jumps, should only be used in an experienced partnership. After all, you don't have to adopt every tip in this book.

221. After a bid of 1NT or 2NT, a leap to 4♣ asks for aces (Gerber). To ask for kings, bid 5♣. Gerber is generally used with powerful long suits, not balanced hands.

Opener	Responder		Opener	Responder
♠KQJ3	♠2		1NT	4♣
♥J42	♥KQ109876		4♥	Pass
♦A103	♦KQ42			
♣KQ7	♣8			

Responder asks for aces, and opener shows one ace. Responder passes, knowing the opponents have three aces!

223. If the Gerber bidder bids 4NT after receiving a response to 4♣, he is not making an "honesty check" by reasking for aces. He is saying that he wants to play the hand in 4NT — two aces are missing!

74

Opener	Responder	Opener	Responder
♠QJ8	♠2	2NT *	4♣
♥AKQJ	♥32	4♥	4NT
♦Q32	♦AKJ10987	Pass	
♣KQJ	♣75		

(*20-22 HCP)

Responder checks for aces, and once again, finds that two are missing. Rather than play at the five level in diamonds, responder opts to play at the four level in notrump.

224. Bid conservatively with "aceless wonders." Bid aggressively with solid suits.

You hold: (a) ♠KQ4 ♥K4 ♦2 ♣KQ109875
         (b) ♠A104 ♥43 ♦2 ♣AKQ10876

South (you)	North
1♣	1♦
?	

With (a), rebid 2♣.
With (b), rebid 3♣.

Avoid making jump bids with aceless wonders.

225. After you open 1NT or 2NT and partner invites with 4NT, pass with a minimum. However, if you have a maximum with a four card minor, show it *en route*.

You hold: ♠K65 ♥A98 ♦AQ65 ♣A76

South (you)	North
1NT (15-17)	4NT
?	

Bid 5♦ to show a maximum, plus a four card diamond suit. If partner also has four diamonds, the hand should play easier in diamonds than notrump. (See next tip.)

226. There is no bridge law stating that you must use Blackwood in order to arrive at a slam. Two balanced hands facing each other seldom, if ever, use Blackwood.

In addition, the opponents may occasionally preempt you beyond the level of 4NT. If you feel there is a good chance for a slam, bid it. You score the same points in the plus column whether or not you use Blackwood.

Opener	Responder	Opener	Responder
♠K65	♠A8	1NT	4NT (invitational)
♥A98	♥KQ4	5♦ (natural)	6♦
♦AQ65	♦KJ32	Pass	
♣A76	♣K843		

These two hands have a combined count of 33 HCP. A contract of 6NT depends upon a 3-3 club division. A contract of 6♦ is virtually laydown. The extra trick comes from a spade ruff.

227. When there are 34-36 HCP between the two balanced hands, 6NT should be the preferred contract, even if there is a 4-4 fit. 6NT usually makes on power, and you need not worry about an obscene trump division.

THINKING OF PREEMPTING?
- Tips 228-242

228. Do not open with a beneath game preempt holding two aces or one ace and two kings. You have too much defensive strength.

229. Vulnerable vs. not, your suit should contain three of the top five honors.

230. After you preempt and partner bids a new suit beneath the game level, you cannot pass!

You hold: ♠3 ♥KJ109874 ♦QJ9 ♣102

South (you)	North
3♥	4♣
?	

Whatever you do, don't pass! 4♣ is forcing. Rebid 4♥; your hearts look pretty good.

231. After a three level minor suit preempt, try to show a side stopper beneath 3NT if partner makes a forcing response.

You hold: ♠QJ4 ♥32 ♦2 ♣AJ108764

South (you)	North
3♣	3♦
?	

Bid 3♠ to show a spade stopper. You can't have a spade suit (See next tip.)

232. Do not preempt in a minor with a side four card major.

You hold: ♠KQ54 ♥3 ♦2 ♣A1098765

As dealer, pass.

233. Do not preempt in one major holding four cards in the other ... unless your suit can play easily opposite a singleton.

You hold: (a) ♠A1087654 ♥K543 ♦2 ♣9
(b) ♠KQJ10765 ♥Q876 ♦3 ♣5

With (a), pass. Your long suit is not independent and preempting in spades may lose a heart fit.
With (b), open 3♠ (or even 4♠ not vulnerable vs. vulnerable). Your spades are so strong that it won't matter if you miss a heart fit.

234. Do not open with a three bid if your hand qualifies for an opening four bid. Most hands with eight card suits or 7-4 distribution open four as opposed to three.

You hold: (a) ♠AQJ10764 ♥3 ♦QJ93 ♣3
(b) ♠KQJ98765 ♥3 ♦4 ♣Q109

Both of these hands open 4♠, not 3♠.

235. Position is important when preempting. First and second seat preempts show traditional values; third seat preempts are suspect because partner has already passed and the preempter is allowed to stretch. Fourth seat preempts are the next thing to opening bids. With a weak hand in fourth seat, pass the hand out.

You hold: ♠3 ♥K54 ♦KJ108764 ♣J7

Open 3♦ in first, second or third seat; pass in fourth seat.

236. A fourth seat opening of 3♣ or 3♦ invites partner to bid 3NT. The opener usually has a solid suit.

You hold: ♠4 ♥654 ♦AKQ10987 ♣K4

In first, second or third seat, open 1♦. In fourth seat, open 3♦.

237. A response of 3NT to a three level preempt ends the auction.

You hold: ♠1072 ♥QJ108765 ♦KJ5 ♣ —

South (you)	North
3♥	3NT
?	

Pass. It's no longer on your head.

238. Preempt as often as possible consistent with the vulnerability. Preempts drive the opponents mad.

239. After you preempt, partner is in charge and takes the sacrifices, not you! Reread this one.

Not vulnerable vs. vulnerable, you hold:

♠4 ♥KQJ10876 ♦J109 ♣87

South (you)	West	North	East
3♥	3♠	4♥	4♠
?			

Even thinking of bidding 5♥ is too shameful to discuss in public. Pass. Your hand is known, but partner's is not. What about the vulnerability? Partner knows about that, too, and may be frothing at the mouth to double.

240. When a preemptive bidder doubles an eventual contract (usually a slam), it generally indicates a side suit void. The double forbids the lead of the preempter's suit and asks (begs) partner for a ruff.

You hold: ♠AJ109742 ♥643 ♦- ♣J107

South (you)	West	North	East
3♠	4♥	Pass	4NT
Pass	5♥	Pass	6♥
?			

Double, and pray.

241. Say you open 3♥ and partner raises to 5♥. What does it mean? It means partner wants to play in 6♥ if your trump suit can play for one loser opposite a small doubleton.

You hold: (a) ♠QJ109876 ♥ — ♦KJ8 ♣32
(b) ♠KQJ8765 ♥43 ♦43 ♣32

South	West	North	East
3♠	Pass	5♠	Pass
?			

With (a), pass. You have two trump losers.
With (b), bid 6♠. You have one trump loser.

242. After you open 4♥ or 4♠ and partner raises to the five level, partner is asking you to bid six if your suit can play opposite a singleton for one loser. If it can't, pass.

You hold: (a) ♠QJ1098765 ♥ – ♦KQ5 ♣87
          (b) ♠KQJ98765 ♥2 ♦54 ♣65

Opener (you)	Responder
4♠	5♠
?	

With (a), pass. You have the same two trump losers.
With (b), bid 6♠. You should be off the ♠A, period.

WHEN THEY PREEMPT - Tips 243-254

243. Be aggressive over enemy preempts with a singleton in their suit. Double with as few as 12 HCP with 4-4-4-1 distribution. With a doubleton in the opponent's suit, look at your support for the unbid major(s). With four card support, double with as few as 14 HCP. With only three card support, double with 15 + HCP.

You hold: (a) ♠AJ104 ♥5 ♦KJ104 ♣K1087
          (b) ♠Q842 ♥32 ♦KQ84 ♣AK3
          (c) ♠Q84 ♥32 ♦AJ98 ♣AQ94

          East   South (you)
          3♥   ?

With (a) or (b), double. With (c), pass.

244. Assume partner has between 4-8 HCP when considering a bid over an enemy preempt. If you don't, you will be afraid to compete.

245. An overcall of a preemptive bid shows opening bid values. A jump over a preempt is strong. With a preemptive hand of your own, pass for the time being.

You hold: (a) ♠AQ10943 ♥A2 ♦QJ6 ♣43
          (b) ♠AKJ1087 ♥2 ♦AQJ9 ♣32
          (c) ♠KQ108765 ♥42 ♦Q6 ♣87

          East   South (you)
          3♣   ?

With (a), bid 3♠.
With (b), bid 4♠.
With (c), pass.

246. A sensible defense to three level preempts is to play "double" shows a three-suited hand, a cuebid, a two-suited hand, and bidding or jumping, a one-suiter.

247. If your right hand opponent opens 3♣ or 3♦, a cuebid of 4♣ or 4♦ is a takeout for the majors. It shows 5-5 or 6-5 distribution with a hand you would have opened.

You hold: (a) ♠KQ1087 ♥AJ9876 ♦4 ♣7
         (b) ♠QJ876 ♥K87643 ♦8 ♣9

East	South (you)
3♦	?

With (a), bid 4♦.
With (b), pass.

248. If your right hand opponent opens 3♥, overcall 4♥ to show spades plus an unknown minor. This cuebid also shows 5-5 or 6-5 distribution with opening bid values.

You hold: ♠AJ1043 ♥3 ♦AKJ876 ♣3

East	South (you)
3♥	?

Bid 4♥. Partner bids 4NT to ask for your minor.

249. The double of an opening 4♥ bid is takeout oriented. The doubler *must* have at least three spades. An overcall of 4NT shows the minors.

You hold: (a) ♠A2 ♥KQ5 ♦A8765 ♣Q98
         (b) ♠A32 ♥4 ♦KQ87 ♣AK876
         (c) ♠3 ♥5 ♦AJ876 ♣AQ10965

East	South (you)
4♥	?

With (a), pass. Don't double. Look at your spades!
With (b), double.
With (c), overcall 4NT.

*250. How should you deal with an opening 4♠ bid? Good question. The tip from here is to double with either a three suited hand short in spades or a strong balanced hand. Overcall 4NT to show a wild two-suiter, and cuebid 5♠ to show "an-end-of-the-world" three-suiter. Do not double simply because you have spade strength. Pass with strong spades and hope partner reopens with a double.

You hold: (a) ♠4 ♥AQ76 ♦KQ54 ♣AK32
    (b) ♠AK92 ♥3 ♦A765 ♣J1043
    (c) ♠543 ♥AK7 ♦AQ4 ♣AJ94
    (d) ♠ — ♥KQ876 ♦AQJ987 ♣K2
    (e) ♠4 ♥3 ♦KQ10876 ♣AKJ65
    (f) ♠ — ♥AKJ4 ♦AQJ87 ♣AKQ4

East	South (you)
4♠	?

With (a), double.
With (b), pass. It only hurts for a little while.
With (c), double.
With (d), bid 4NT. If partner bids 5♣, bid 5♦ to show the reds.
With (e), bid 4NT.
With (f), bid 5♠. Don't worry; you'll never hold this hand.

251. When partner doubles a game preempt, pass with most balanced hands and remove with distributional hands.

You hold: (a) ♠A76 ♥543 ♦QJ54 ♣Q108
    (b) ♠A76 ♥543 ♦QJ8765 ♣3

West	North	East	South (you)
4♥	Double	Pass	?

With (a), pass.
With (b), bid 5♦.

252. The time to become aggressive is when a three level preempt is passed around to you and you have a singleton in the opponent's suit with support for the other suits. Double with as little as 10 HCP. With a doubleton in the opponent's suit and support for the unbid major(s), double with as few as 11 or 12 HCP. With three cards in their suit, you need 15-16 HCP to reopen with a double.

You hold: (a) ♠AJ92 ♥43 ♦QJ76 ♣K87
    (b) ♠AJ5 ♥632 ♦Q876 ♣AQ4
    (c) ♠AJ98 ♥5 ♦KQ87 ♣9976

West	North	East	South (you)
3♥	Pass	Pass	?

With (a), double.
With (b), pass.
With (c), double.

253. Are you ready for this one? An overcall of 3NT after a three level preempt has a range of 16-22!

You hold: (a) ♠AQ ♥Q87 ♦AQJ9 ♣J1087
        (b) ♠AKJ ♥A87 ♦KQ76 ♣AJ2

East	South (you)
3♠	?

Overcall 3NT with both hands! How will partner know? He won't!

254. Preempts with very light hands are the rage these days. Be prepared for three level preempts on six card suits, etc. Third seat non-vulnerable preempts, in particular, tend to be light. Forewarned is forearmed.

84

WHEN YOU ARE A PASSED HAND
- Tips 255-268

255. A new suit response to an opening bid is not forcing. If you wish to force, jump shift. A jump shift is a one round force, not a game force.

*256. A jump shift promises primary support for opener's suit. It does not show an "almost opening bid" without primary support. It can be made with a four card suit.

You hold: (a) ♠AK876 ♥K87 ♦J76 ♣32
            (b) ♠AKJ4 ♥4 ♦43 ♣Q108765

South (you)	North
Pass	1♣
?	

With (a), bid 1♠. A jump to 2♠ promises at least four, and usually five, clubs.
With (b), bid 2♠.

257. A jump in a new suit in response to an overcall shows a two-suited hand — the suit you are bidding and partner's suit.

You hold: ♠KQ1043 ♥2 ♦54 ♣A10876

South (you)	West	North	East
Pass	1♥	2♣	2♥
?			

Bid 3♠ to show a spade-club two-suiter.

*258. A jump one level higher than a jump shift is a splinter jump.

You hold: ♠A54 ♥3 ♦QJ8765 ♣K42

South (you)	North
Pass	1♦
?	

Bid 3♥. Your jump shows a massive diamond fit, a singleton heart, and 9-11 HCP. Perfect. With a preempt in hearts, you would have opened 3♥.

259. A direct overcall of 1NT after a major suit opening bid is "unusual" for the minors. It shows 5-5 or 6-5 distribution with 7-10 HCP.

You hold: ♠4 ♥5 ♦QJ8765 ♣AQ765

South (you)	West	North	East
Pass	Pass	Pass	1♠
?			

Bid 1NT. As a non-passed hand, jump to 2NT to show the minors. A 1NT overcall would be natural.

260. A 1NT overcall of a minor suit opening bid is also "unusual." It shows hearts plus the other minor (5-5 or 6-5) with 7-10 HCP.

You hold: ♠4 ♥K8765 ♦5 ♣A87654

South (you)	West	North	East
Pass	Pass	Pass	1♦
?			

Overcall 1NT to show the two lower unbids.

261. There is no such animal as a direct overcall of 1NT to show a balanced hand. All direct notrump overcalls are unusual.

You hold: ♠A104 ♥KJ9 ♦Q1042 ♣J98

South (you)	West	North	East
Pass	Pass	Pass	1♥
?			

Pass. Do not even think of bidding 1NT. You would be showing a minor two-suiter!

262. Balancing 1NT bids are natural and show 10-12 HCP.

You hold: ♠A104 ♥KJ9 ♦Q1042 ♣J98

South (you)	West	North	East
Pass	1♥	Pass	Pass
?			

Reopen with 1NT, natural. You are in the balancing seat.

263. A balancing 2NT bid is "unusual." After a major suit opening, it shows the minors. After a minor suit opening, it shows hearts plus the other minor, 7-10 HCP.

264. Avoid a two level response on a four card suit. Partner may pass with a small doubleton in your suit. You will not be a happy camper playing a 4-2 fit.

You hold: ♠32 ♥KJ5 ♦AK87 ♣5432

South (you)	North
Pass	1♥
?	

Assuming you don't play "Drury," respond 3♥ rather than 2♦. The risk of being dropped in 2♦ is greater than the one trump you owe partner for your jump.

265. A 2NT response shows 11-12 balanced and *denies* a singleton. A one or two level response followed by 2NT shows the same strength but may contain a singleton.

You hold: (a) ♠76 ♥AJ5 ♦KJ43 ♣Q1054
(b) ♠7 ♥AJ43 ♦KJ4 ♣Q8765

South (you)	North
Pass	1♠
?	

With (a), respond 2NT.
With (b), respond 2♣ and rebid 2NT if partner rebids 2♠ or 2♦.

266. There is no such animal as a nautural response of 3NT unless you missorted or miscounted your hand.

267. With 4-4-4-1 shape, double with as few as 9 HCP if the opponents open your short suit.

You hold: (a) ♠KJ43 ♥5 ♦K1054 ♣Q976
(b) ♠KJ43 ♥65 ♦K876 ♣Q76
(c) ♠KJ3 ♥J654 ♦A876 ♣Q8

South (you)	West	North	East
Pass	Pass	Pass	1♥
?			

With (a), double.
With (b), double.
With (c), pass - four cards in their suit.

268. With any 4-4-3-2 distribution, double with 9-11 HCP if your right hand opponent opens the bidding in your short suit. If your right hand opponent opens your three card suit, double with 9-11, providing you are 4-4 in the unbid majors. If your right hand opponent opens one of your four card suits, pass.

*269. After an intervening overcall, the cuebid substitutes for the limit raise. The jump raise becomes preemptive. This idea is both popular and effective.

You hold: (a) ♠87 ♥K10876 ♦Q1054 ♣32
(b) ♠87 ♥AQ87 ♦KJ104 ♣J32

South (you)	West	North	East
Pass	Pass	1♥	2♣
?			

With (a), bid 3♥, preemptive.
With (b), bid 3♣, a limit raise in hearts.

AFTER PARTNER OPENS 1NT
- Tips 270-284

270. Do not bother using Stayman with 4-3-3-3 or 3-4-3-3 distribution.

271. You need at least 8 HCP to use Stayman. If you do not connect in a major and are forced to retreat to 2NT, partner will play you for 8-9 HCP.

You hold: (a) ♠A876 ♥Q753 ♦53 ♣1065
(b) ♠AJ43 ♥K1043 ♦43 ♣987

North	South (you)
1NT (15-17)	?

With (a), pass. You are not strong enough to launch into a Stayman sequence. Partner may rebid 2♦; then what?
With (b), bid 2♣. If partner rebids 2♦, rebid 2NT without being ashamed of your dummy.

272. With a three-suited hand short in *clubs*, you can use Stayman with a bust. You are planning to pass any rebid partner makes, including 2♦.

You hold: ♠Q1054 ♥J987 ♦109876 ♣-

North	South (you)
1NT	?

Respond 2♣ and pass anything partner bids.

273. If your right hand opponent makes a two level overcall, a three level cuebid is Stayman.

You hold: (a) ♠K876 ♥32 ♦J54 ♣AQ98
(b) ♠643 ♥Q8 ♦2 ♣K1098763

North	East	South (you)	West
1NT	2♥	?	

With (a), bid 3♥ Stayman.
With (b), bid 3♣, natural and not forcing.

*274. If your right hand opponent makes a three level overcall, "double" replaces Stayman. If you wish to make a penalty double, you can't. Either pass or bid 3NT. You can't have your cake and eat it, too.

You hold: (a) ♠AJ43 ♥42 ♦K1075 ♣Q43
(b) ♠75 ♥KJ93 ♦43 ♣J8765

North	East	South (you)	West
1NT	3♥	?	

With (a), double (Stayman). Partner can either bid 3♠ with four spades, pass with good hearts or bid 3NT.
With (b), pass. Sorry.

275. If you are not using transfer responses to notrump opening bids, reconsider. It is important that the stronger hand becomes the declarer.

276. If the opponents play that a double of partner's 1NT opening bid shows an *unknown* one-suited hand, ignore the double and play 2♣ as Stayman, etc.

277. If the opponents play that an overcall of 2♣ shows an *unknown* one-suiter, double is Stayman and everything else retains its original meaning.

278. If the opponents play that a double of 1NT is for penalty, any bid by you at the two level, including 2♣, shows weakness with length; redouble to show 8 or more HCP.

279. If the opponents play that a double of 1NT is for penalty, no Stayman. If you are strong enough to use Stayman, you are strong enough to redouble.

280. Do not run from 1NT doubled with a balanced hand. Stick it out; fourth hand might run.

You hold: (a) ♠J876 ♥54 ♦10976 ♣J32
(b) ♠J876 ♥54 ♦109765 ♣32

North	East	South (you)	West
1NT	Double*	?	

*Penalty

With (a), pass. You won't have to play the hand; partner will.
With (b), run to 2♦.

281. A direct raise to 4NT is natural; a 2♣ response followed by 4NT is also natural.

You hold: (a) ♠AJ ♥Q104 ♦K8765 ♣AJ10
(b) ♠AJ ♥Q1042 ♦K876 ♣AQ5

North	South (you)
1NT	?

With (a), bid 4NT.
With (b), bid 2♣. If partner rebids 2♦ or 2♠, rebid 4NT, natural.

282. After a Stayman response, if you wish to ask for aces, jump to 4♣. This is one of the few times 4♣ is used to ask for aces when the previous bid is not 1NT or 2NT.

You hold: ♠KQ76 ♥4 ♦KQ765 ♣KJ9

North	South (you)
1NT	2♣
2♠	?

Jump to 4♣ to ask for aces.

283. With a six card minor headed by two of the top three honors and 7-11 HCP, leap to 3NT. Do not bid the minor suit.

You hold: (a) ♠4 ♥876 ♦AKJ987 ♣432
(b) ♠J4 ♥32 ♦765 ♣AQJ987

North	South (you)
1NT	?

Raise to 3NT.

284. A jump response promises at least a six card suit. Stayman followed by a major suit rebid shows a five card suit.

You hold: (a) ♠AQ876 ♥K4 ♦876 ♣K104
         (b) ♠AQ8765 ♥K4 ♦876 ♣Q104

North	South (you)
1NT	?

Assuming you don't play transfers, bid 2♣ with (a), and then bid 2♠ if you play Forcing Stayman, 3♠, if you do not.
With (b), jump to 3♠ to show a six card suit.

AFTER PARTNER RESPONDS 2♣ TO YOUR OPENING 1NT BID
- Tips 285-288

*285. If you believe in opening 1NT with a five card major or a six card minor, jump to the three level to let partner in on the secret.

You hold: (a) ♠A2 ♥AQ1054 ♦K75 ♣K42
(b) ♠K2 ♥K2 ♦AQ8765 ♣K107

South (you)	North
1NT	2♣
?	

With (a), bid 3♥.
With (b), bid 3♦.

286. With no four card major, rebid 2♦. Do not rebid 2NT.

*287. With two four card majors, bid the *stronger* one first. If partner rebids 3NT, bid the other major. If partner rebids 2NT, rebid three of the other major with a *minimum*; four of the other major with a *maximum*. This tip assumes that when partner bids 2♣ followed by 2NT or 3NT, it promises at least one major suit.

You hold: (a) ♠AQJ7 ♥J843 ♦AQ4 ♣K7
(b) ♠AQJ7 ♥Q843 ♦KJ4 ♣Q9

South (you)	North
1NT (15-17)	2♣
2♠	2NT
?	

With (a), bid 4♥.
With (b), bid 3♥. Had partner rebid 3NT, bid 4♥ with either hand.

Some players always bid hearts first. The reason for bidding the stronger one first is that if partner also has both majors, you wind up in the stronger trump suit.

93

288. If your right hand opponent doubles:

(1) Bid a four card major if you have one.
(2) If you do not have a four card major but you do have a club stopper, pass.
(3) If you do not have a four card major and you do not have a club stopper, bid 2♦.
(4) If you have four or five wonderful clubs, redouble.

You hold: (a) ♠AJ87 ♥K87 ♦A98 ♣A87
          (b) ♠AJ9 ♥K76 ♦AKJ3 ♣876
          (c) ♠AJ9 ♥K76 ♦KJ43 ♣A87
          (d) ♠A10 ♥K76 ♦AJ4 ♣QJ987

South (you)	West	North	East
1NT	Pass	2♣	Double
?			

With (a), bid 2♠.
With (b), bid 2♦ - No four card major, no club stopper.
With (c), pass - No four card major, but a club stopper.
With (d), redouble. You are more than willing to play 2♣ doubled and redoubled.

FOUR NOTRUMP - Tips 289-296

289. 4NT is *not* always Blackwood. Wait, do not burn this book! 4NT can be Blackwood; it can be a takeout for the minors; it can be a three-suited takeout; it can be a two suited takeout; it can be natural. It all depends upon the previous bidding. Now you can burn the book.

290. After either player bids 1NT or 2NT, and is raised by partner to 4NT, the 4NT bid is *natural and not forcing*. To ask for aces in these sequences, jump to 4♣, Gerber. If you don't use Gerber, now is a good time to start.

291. After the fourth suit by either the opener or the responder, 4NT is natural. The range is 18-19 HCP.

(a) | Opener | Responder | (b) | Opener | Responder |
|---|---|---|---|---|
| 1♠ | 2♦ | | 1♦ | 1♥ |
| 2♥ | 3♣ (4th suit) | | 2♦ | 2♠ |
| 4NT (natural) | | | 3♣(4th suit) | 4NT (natural) |

292. After a two-over-one response and a 3NT rebid by the opener, 4NT by responder is natural.

Opener	Responder
1♠	2♦
3NT	4NT (natural)

293. In the absence of more sophisticated agreements, leap to 5♣ over 3NT to ask for aces.

294. In each of the following sequences, the final 4NT bid is a minor suit takeout.

(a) | West | North | East | South |
|---|---|---|---|
| 1♥ | Pass | 3♥/4♥ | 4NT |

(b) | West | North | East | South |
|---|---|---|---|
| 2♥* | Pass | 3♥/4♥ | 4NT |

*Weak

(c)	West	North	East	South
	3♥	Pass	4♥	4NT

(d)	West	North	East	South
	3♥/4♥	Pass	Pass	4NT

If East-West had been bidding spades instead of hearts, 4NT would carry the same meaning.

295. After partner opens 1♣ or 1♦ and second hand overcalls 4♠, 4NT is for takeout.

You hold: (a) ♠4 ♥KQ87 ♦AJ987 ♣AJ9
          (b) ♠4 ♥AJ1065 ♦AK7654 ♣4

North	East	South (you)	West
1♣	4♠	?	

Bid 4NT with both hands. If partner bids 5♣, pass with (a) and bid 5♦ with (b) to show diamonds and hearts. No Blackwood after a minor suit opening and a 4♠ overcall.

296. Here's a dynamite tip: Use an opening bid of 4NT to ask for *specific* aces. With no aces, partner responds 5♣; with one ace, partner bids the suit in which the ace is held. Holding the ♣A, partner responds 6♣. With two aces (don't hold your breath), partner responds 5NT. This opening bid is reserved for powerful freak hands that contain a void.

You hold: ♠AKQ98543 ♥KQJ2 ♦A ♣ –

Open 4NT! If partner responds 5♥, bid 7♠. If partner responds 5NT, bid 7NT. If partner responds 5♣ or 6♣, sign off in 6♠. With a bit of luck, you may get to use this bid once in your life, perhaps.

WHEN YOU MAKE A
NEGATIVE DOUBLE - Tips 297-322

297. Negative doubles do not follow all inclusive rules. What they show depends upon the level and which two suits are unbid.

298. Only the responder can make a negative double, and it must be made at the first opportunity.

299. In theory, a negative double denies six cards in an unbid major suit.

300. Doubling and then bidding a major suit presumes a five card suit. Doubling and then bidding a minor suit can show either a five or six card suit.

You hold: ♠876 ♥A765 ♦K109843 ♣-

North	East	South (you)	West
1♣	1♠	Double	Pass
2♣	Pass	2♦	

The 2♦ bid shows diamond length and a hand not strong enough to respond 2♦ originally. It also promises four hearts.

301. Negative doubles at the one and two levels with five and six card suits are limited. They show fewer than 10 HCP. With 10 + HCP, bid the long suit directly. Think of a negative double followed by a suit as if partner were trying to put brakes on the bidding sequence.

*302. When *one* major suit is unbid, a negative double at the one or two level promises four card support for that major.

North	East	South (you)	West
1♣/♦	1♥	Double	

You promise exactly four spades. A 1♠ response shows at least five spades. Some play that the double denies four spades.

303. Negative doubles with *four* card suits are *unlimited*. At the one level, they promise a minimum of 6 HCP. In the previous tip, you could have any strength hand for your double.

304. When both minors have been bid at the *one* level, "double" promises four cards in each of the unbid majors or five hearts and four spades with 6-9 HCP.

You hold: (a) ♠AJ87 ♥KQ76 ♦54 ♣A76
         (b) ♠AJ87 ♥K43 ♦543 ♣987
         (c) ♠AJ965 ♥KQ76 ♦43 ♣32
         (d) ♠AQ32 ♥108765 ♦43 ♣J6

North	East	South (you)	West
1♣	1♦	?	

With (a), double. You have four cards in each unbid major.
With (b), bid 1♠.
With (c), bid 1♠. No negative doubles with five card *spade* suits at the *one* level.
With (d), double. If you respond 1♥, you may lose a spade fit if fourth hand bids.

305. When both minors have been mentioned at the two or three level, "double" either shows at least four card support for both unbid majors or four card support for one major plus *primary* support for opener's suit. Reread this one.

You hold: (a) ♠AQ76 ♥K1043 ♦43 ♣765
         (b) ♠J987 ♥43 ♦43 ♣AK1065
         (c) ♠Q1043 ♥43 ♦8765 ♣AQ2

North	East	South (you)	West
1♣	2♦	?	

With (a), double. Perfect.
With (b), double. If partner bids hearts, return to clubs.
With (c), pass. You have no place to go if partner bids 2♥. A return to partner's suit is supposed to show four card support.

306. When both majors have been bid, "double" promises at least four cards in each of the unbid minors.

(a) **North**   **East**   **South**   (b) **North**   **East**   **South**
    1♥   1♠   Double   1♥   2♠   Double

The double shows support for both minors. Exceptionally, South may have long diamonds, 7-9 HCP, i.e., ♠42 ♥K3 ♦Q87432 ♣K105.

307. The lower the level of the negative double, the more precise the requirements. Many negative doubles made at the three and four levels simply say, "I have a good hand with no long suit and no great support for your suit. Save me!"

You hold: ♠765 ♥54 ♦AK87 ♣AJ87

        North   **East**   **South** (you)   **West**
          1♥   3♠   ?

Double — what else can you do? You can't let them steal you blind, and you have no long suit to bid.

308. A negative double at the two level shows a minimum of 8 HCP. A negative double at the three level shows a minimum of 10 HCP.

309. When counting points, do not include jacks and queens in the opponent's suit - unless you are intending to rebid notrump, or are a masochist.

310. A big problem is how to handle a five card major suit that must be shown at the two level. Bid the suit with 10+ HCP, double with 7-9 HCP.

You hold: (a) ♠65 ♥AKJ87 ♦Q54 ♣1087
              (b) ♠765 ♥AQ987 ♦Q4 ♣1065

        North   **East**   **South** (you)   **West**
          1♦   1♠   ?

With (a), bid 2♥. Just strong enough.
With (b), double and hope to bid hearts at the two level, denying the strength for a direct 2♥ response.

311. In competition, six card major suits can be shown at the two level with as few as 8 HCP.

You hold: (a) ♠K4 ♥AJ10432 ♦87 ♣987
           (b) ♠87 ♥Q87654 ♦K4 ♣Q87

North	East	South (you)	West
1♣	1♠	?	

With (a), bid 2♥.
With (b), double and hope to bid 2♥, even though partner will play you for a five card suit (an exception).

312. A negative double followed by a new suit is not forcing. In order to create a force, cuebid.

You hold: ♠AKJ4 ♥KQ104 ♦87 ♣876

North	East	South (you)	West
1♣	2♦	Double	Pass
3♣	Pass	?	

Bid 3♦ to create a force. If you bid a major, you are showing a five (or six) card suit and 7-9 HCP. Not exactly what you have.

313. A negative double followed by a raise of partner's second suit is not forcing.

You hold: (a) ♠A4 ♥AJ76 ♦Q1043 ♣876
           (b) ♠A4 ♥AJ76 ♦KJ104 ♣876

North	East	South (you)	West
1♣	1♠	Double	Pass
2♥	Pass	?	

With (a), raise to 3♥, invitational.
With (b), raise to 4♥. The one who knows, goes.

314. A negative double followed by a 2NT rebid shows 10-12 HCP and is not forcing.

You hold: (a) ♠A104 ♥QJ87 ♦A10 ♣5432
           (b) ♠AJ4 ♥QJ87 ♦AQ ♣5432

North	East	South (you)	West
1♣	1♠	Double	2♠
Pass	Pass	?	

With (a), bid 2NT, invitational.
With (b), bid 3NT. The one who knows, goes.

315. If, after you make a negative double, your left hand opponent raises, and the bidding comes back dead to you, a repeat double is also for takeout, showing extra strength.

You hold: ♠AQ76 ♥654 ♦KJ43 ♣104

North	East	South (you)	West
1♣	1♥	Double	2♥
Pass	Pass	?	

Double again to show 10 + HCP.

316. When most of your strength is in the opponent's suit, avoid a negative double. It is very misleading. Either bid notrump or pass. Reread this one.

You hold: (a) ♠10876 ♥AQ104 ♦J4 ♣J103
           (b) ♠10876 ♥KQJ4 ♦87 ♣983

North	East	South (you)	West
1♦	1♥	?	

With (a), respond 1NT, showing 8-10 HCP.
With (b), pass. It would be a blunder to double with this hand, even though you have four spades. It would also be a blunder to respond 1NT. You are not strong enough. Patience is a great virtue.

317. If you pass a one level overcall and partner reopens with a takeout double, a 1NT response shows 5-7 HCP. It is weaker than a direct response of 1NT. See (b) in the previous tip. If partner reopens with a double, bid 1NT. A 1♠ response is also possible.

101

318. When you play negative doubles, you cannot make an immediate penalty double. With a strong five or six card holding in the opponent's suit, don't gasp, just pass. It is *mega* important to pass ethically so partner is not aware of your great strength.

You hold: (a) ♠742 ♥AK1098 ♦3 ♣Q987
(b) ♠6432 ♥KQJ976 ♦3 ♣A8

North	East	South (you)	West
1♦	1♥	?	

With both hands, pass. If partner reopens with a double, pass again.

319. Assume partner opens, your right hand opponent overcalls, you pass, and your left hand opponent bids a new suit which is passed back to you. If you bid your *right hand opponent's* suit, that bid is natural and not forcing.

You hold: ♠984 ♥KQ10964 ♦Q7 ♣J9

North	East	South (you)	West
1♦	1♥	Pass	2♣
Pass	Pass	?	

Bid 2♥.

320. A delayed double after both opponents bid is a penalty double of right hand opponent's suit! It also shows 10+ HCP with some strength outside of your right hand opponent's suit.

You hold: ♠J76 ♥AQ1054 ♦A4 ♣876

North	East	South (you)	West
1♦	1♥	Pass	2♣
Pass	Pass	?	

Double, telling partner (1) that you have hearts, (2) that the hand belongs to your side and (3), to do something intelligent, for once.

321. A delayed double after left hand opponent raises, is a penalty double.

You hold: ♠975 ♥65 ♦AJ104 ♣K876

North	East	South	West
1♥	2♦	Pass	3♦
Pass	Pass	?	

Double — this one says that you have diamonds. Finally!

322. A negative double with three cards in partner's major is rare. Do not even consider doing it with less than 11 HCP. Even then, you are going to have to jump to confirm the support. Partner is not expecting three card major suit support when you double.

You hold: ♠AJ4 ♥8765 ♦KQ4 ♣QJ3

North	East	South (you)	West
1♠	2♥	?	

Double and then jump in spades to show this awkward hand.

103

REBIDDING AFTER PARTNER MAKES A NEGATIVE DOUBLE - Tips 323-331

323. With a minimum hand, make a minimum rebid. With an invitational hand, make a jump rebid. With a game-going hand, bid game or cuebid.

*324. After partner doubles a 1♥ overcall, rebid as if partner had responded 1♠ on a four card suit with at least 6 HCP — although he could have much more. If he does, you'll hear about it soon enough.

You hold: (a) ♠A432 ♥K74 ♦32 ♣AJ98
           (b) ♠A432 ♥74 ♦32 ♣AKQ32
           (c) ♠AQ84 ♥74 ♦K4 ♣AK732
           (d) ♠AQ84 ♥74 ♦A4 ♣AK732
           (e) ♠74 ♥AQ4 ♦J43 ♣AJ987
           (f) ♠743 ♥AQ4 ♦K43 ♣AKQ4
           (g) ♠7 ♥A54 ♦AKJ4 ♣KQ765
           (h) ♠74 ♥Q5 ♦Q765 ♣AKQ76
           (i) ♠KQ54 ♥A76 ♦2 ♣AK987

South (you)	West	North	East
1♣	1♥	Double	Pass
?			

With (a), bid 1♠, the weakest spade bid possible, showing 12-14 support points.
With (b), bid 2♠, showing 15-16 support points.
With (c), bid 3♠, showing 17-18 support points.
With (d), bid 4♠, showing 19-20 support points.
With (e), bid 1NT.
With (f), bid 2NT.
With (g), bid 2♦, a reverse.
With (h), bid 2♣ - the same bid you would have made over a 1♠ response.
With (i), bid 3♦, a splinter.

This is not the mainstream approach with (g) and (i), but I'll stick by it anyway.

*325. After partner doubles 1♠, rebid as if partner had responded 1♥ on a four card suit.

You hold: (a) ♠KJ4 ♥43 ♦KQ765 ♣A104
           (b) ♠KJ4 ♥43 ♦AK765 ♣AK4
           (c) ♠53 ♥10432 ♦AK74 ♣AJ4
           (d) ♠53 ♥AK74 ♦AK876 ♣98
           (e) ♠A4 ♥AQ87 ♦AK876 ♣J9
           (f) ♠4 ♥54 ♦AK876 ♣AQ987
           (g) ♠4 ♥54 ♦AKQ87 ♣AKQ108

South (you)	West	North	East
1♦	1♠	Double	Pass
?			

With (a), bid 1NT.
With (b), bid 2NT.
With (c), bid 2♥.
With (d), bid 3♥.
With (e), bid 4♥.
With (f), bid 2♣. Partner has not promised clubs, just four hearts.
With (g), bid 3♣ - a game force. Most play a jump shift invitational in this sequence.

326. After partner doubles 1♦, showing at least four cards in each major (possibly five hearts and four spades), jump bids in the majors are invitational.

You hold: (a) ♠A1042 ♥43 ♦765 ♣AKJ4
           (b) ♠AQ42 ♥4 ♦865 ♣AK432
           (c) ♠AQ104 ♥Q4 ♦32 ♣AKJ84
           (d) ♠94 ♥AKQ4 ♦32 ♣AKJ94

South (you)	West	North	East
1♣	1♦	Double	Pass
?			

With (a), bid 1♠, showing 12-14 support points.
With (b), bid 2♠, showing 15-16 support points.
With (c), bid 3♠, showing 17-18 support points.
With (d), bid 4♥, showing 19-20 support points.

327. After partner doubles a *two* level overcall, the meaning of opener's rebids varies dramatically. 2NT shows 14-16 HCP; 3NT, 17-19. Non-jump bids show minimums; jumps are invitational. The cuebid is a game force.

You hold: (a) ♠AJ932 ♥32 ♦K43 ♣A54
           (b) ♠AJ1043 ♥32 ♦AQ5 ♣K32
           (c) ♠AJ875 ♥A108 ♦Q43 ♣Q5
           (d) ♠AK876 ♥AQ76 ♦43 ♣98
           (e) ♠AK876 ♥AQ43 ♦43 ♣A2
           (f) ♠AKJ10876 ♥2 ♦4 ♣KQ76
           (g) ♠AQJ987 ♥2 ♦A43 ♣KJ10
           (h) ♠AK875 ♥A103 ♦2 ♣AK104
           (i) ♠AK876 ♥AJ43 ♦2 ♣A106
           (j) ♠AK876 ♥32 ♦AK4 ♣QJ9

South (you)	West	North	East
1♠	2♦	Double	Pass
?			

With (a), rebid 2♠ - Not strong enough to rebid 2NT.
With (b), bid 2NT. Perfect.
*With (c), bid 2♥! You are not strong enough to bid 2NT, and it is safer to rebid 2♥, a suit partner must have, rather than 2♠, a suit partner doesn't have. (See tip #322.)
With (d), bid 3♥, invitational.
With (e), bid 4♥. You are too strong to invite.
With (f), bid 4♠. You are too strong to invite with 3♠.
With (g), bid 3♠, invitational.
With (h), bid 3♦, a game-forcing cuebid.
With (i), bid 4♦, a splinter raise of hearts, the one suit partner has promised.
With (j), rebid 3NT.

328. Do not pass a one or two level negative double unless you have both length (at least five cards) and intermediates in the opponent's suit. (Atypically you might pass holding four cards to 100 honors.)

You hold: (a) ♠A4 ♥KQ1043 ♦3 ♣KQ1097
           (b) ♠A4 ♥KQ1054 ♦65 ♣AQ76
           (c) ♠A4 ♥KJ876 ♦43 ♣KQJ10
           (d) ♠A43 ♥A7642 ♦3 ♣KQJ10

South (you)	West	North	East
1♥	2♣	Double	Pass
?			

With (a), pass. You should only be so lucky.
With (b), bid 2NT. Your clubs are not strong enough to pass.
With (c), pass. Even though you only have four clubs, suits with 100 honors are usually treated as one card longer than they actually are.
With (d), pass. Your clubs are good enough.

329. The higher the level of the negative double, the less strength you need in the opponent's suit to pass. With a balanced hand and three cards in the opponent's suit, a pass becomes a viable option.

You hold: (a) ♠AK876 ♥54 ♦A32 ♣K108
(b) ♠AK876 ♥QJ5 ♦32 ♣K87

South (you)	West	North	East
1♠	3♦	Double	Pass
?			

With (a), pass. Partner is presumed short in spades, making your hand attractive defensively.
*With (b), bid 3♥! This one is a little scary. At this level, partner does not promise four hearts, but probably has at least four. It is far too risky to pass. Therefore, your options are 3♥ and 3♠. Nobody ever said playing negative doubles was going to solve all your problems.

330. Big tip coming up: Assume you open the bidding, your left hand opponent overcalls, and there are two passes back to you. If you are short in the opponent's suit (void, singleton or small doubleton), there is a good chance that partner might be lurking over there with a penalty double of the opponent's suit. Ask yourself the following question: If partner had made a penalty double of this overcall, would I have passed? If the answer is yes, reopen the bidding with a takeout double. If the answer is no, bid something else.

You hold: (a) ♠A876 ♥3 ♦QJ87 ♣KQ54
(b) ♠KQ4 ♥54 ♦A876 ♣KQ76
(c) ♠2 ♥9 ♦AQ10876 ♣KQ987

107

South (you)	West	North	East
1♦	1♥	Pass	Pass
?			

With (a), double. Had partner made a penalty double of 1♥, you would have passed - I hope.

With (b), double - same reason.

With (c), bid 2♣. You would not have passed a penalty double of 1♥.

331. Assume you open the bidding, your left hand opponent overcalls, and there are two passes back to you, and you have length in their suit (three or more cards, or exceptionally, a strong a doubleton). Now it is safe to assume that partner does not have a penalty double of their suit. Therefore, partner should be weak. In order to reopen the bidding with length in the opponent's suit, you need extra values, either high card or distributional.

You hold:. (a) ♠A87 ♥QJ4 ♦AK765 ♣43
(b) ♠A765 ♥QJ76 ♦AKJ4 ♣4
(c) ♠Q1054 ♥A54 ♦AKJ765 ♣-
(d) ♠A76 ♥QJ4 ♦AK108 ♣AJ10

South (you)	West	North	East
1♦	1♥	Pass	Pass
?			

With (a), pass. Nothing plus nothing equals nothing.

With (b), pass. Partner couldn't make a negative double or support diamonds. Where are you going?

With (c), bid 1♠. You can't give up on this hand.

With (d), bid 1NT. A reopening bid of 1NT shows 18-19 HCP.

WHEN YOU DOUBLE AN
ARTIFICIAL BID - Tips 332-355

332. The main reason to double an artificial bid is to invite the lead of that suit.

333. The double of any artificial bid is a penalty double.

334. The double of any low level artificial bid requires either five cards headed by three of the top five honors, or six cards headed by two of the top four honors in the suit. Overcalling the artificial suit, typically at the three level, shows the equivalent of a vulnerable opening three bid.

You hold: (a) ♠43 ♥A76 ♦84 ♣KJ10973
           (b) ♠43 ♥AK6 ♦84 ♣J87654
           (c) ♠4 ♥54 ♦K109 ♣KQJ10543

West	North	East	South (you)
1NT	Pass	2♣	?

With (a), double, you have the length and the strength.
With (b), pass. You have the length, but not the strength.
With (c), overcall 3♣ to show a vulnerable opening 3♣ bid.

335. The double of four level or higher artificial bids requires strength, not length. A three card holding headed by two of the top three honors is enough.

You hold: (a) ♠43 ♥KQ10 ♦8765 ♣10876
           (b) ♠43 ♥Q98765 ♦72 ♣KQ9

West	North	East	South (you)
1♠	Pass	3♠	Pass
4♦	Pass	4♥	?

With (a), double, You want a heart lead vs. a spade contract.
With (b), pass. You do not want to encourage a heart lead; you prefer a club lead.

336. Do not double an artificial bid if you are likely to be on lead unless you suffer from amnesia and need a reminder.

You hold: ♠43 ♥KQJ8 ♦876 ♣10742

East	South (you)	West	North
1♠	Pass	3♠	Pass
4♣	Pass	4♦	Pass
4♥	?		

Pass. Do not double for a heart lead. You will be on lead!

337. To double an artificial bid when you will be on lead hurts your own cause. Not only do you warn your opponents of your strength, but, worse, you give the next hand options not previously available — pass and redouble.

338. The common artificial bids to be on the lookout for are:

(1) Stayman responses to 1NT and 2NT opening bids
(2) Transfer responses to 1NT and 2NT opening bids
(3) Cuebids
(4) Blackwood responses
(5) Splinter bids
(6) Drury

339. When you fail to double a Blackwood response, you warn partner that you have no great interest in that suit being led.

You hold: ♠87 ♥J765 ♦10875 ♣KQJ

West	North	East	South (you)
1♠	Pass	3♠	Pass
4NT	Pass	5♣	?

Seize the opportunity to double. This insures a club lead vs. an eventual spade contract. Passing 5♣ is a bridge blunder!

340. After you double a low level artificial bid and later bid a new suit, you show a two-suited hand.

110

You hold: ♠4 ♥AJ1054 ♦32♣KQJ98

West	North	East	South	(you)
1NT	Pass	2♥*	Double	
2♠	Pass	Pass	3♣	

*Transfer

The double shows long hearts, and the club bid shows long clubs. Voila, you have shown your hand. What a player!

341. Partner's double of 3NT asks for a particular lead. It doesn't hurt to know the rules.

342. If no suits have been bid, partner's double of 3NT announces the possession of some solid suit, usually a major.

You hold: ♠Q765 ♥76 ♦Q5432 ♣87

East	South	West	North
1NT	Pass	3NT	Double

Partner has a solid suit. It can't be spades or diamonds, so it must be hearts or clubs. With a blind choice between a major and a minor, lead the major.

343. When neither you nor your partner has bid, lead dummy's first bid suit.

You hold: ♠84 ♥Q875 ♦QJ932 ♣105

East	South (you)	West	North
1♥	Pass	1♠	Pass
1NT	Pass	2NT	Pass
3NT	Pass	Pass	Double

Don't try to be a genius. Lead the ♠8, as partner requested.

344. If you have *not* bid and partner has overcalled at the two or three level, lead partner's suit.

You hold: ♠J1087 ♥4 ♦96 ♣QJ10543

East	South (you)	West	North
1♠	Pass	2♦	2♥
2NT	Pass	3NT	Double

Lead your singleton heart. The lead of the ♣Q is the equivalent to a slap in partner's face.

*345. If *you* overcall at the one level and partner passes throughout and later doubles 3NT:

(1) If partner had a chance to support your suit at the *two* level after a one level response and did not, lead dummy's first bid suit.

(2) If partner had no chance to support your suit at the two level, lead your suit.

You hold: ♠84 ♥KJ864 ♦AJ10 ♣543

(a) East	South (you)	West	North
1♣	1♥	1♠	Pass
1NT	Pass	2NT	Pass
3NT	Pass	Pass	Double
Pass	Pass	Pass	

(b) East	South (you)	West	North
1♣	1♥	3♣	Pass
3NT	Pass	Pass	Double
Pass	Pass	Pass	

In (a), partner had a chance to support you at the two level and did not. Lead the ♠8.

In (b), partner had no chance to support you at the two level. Lead the ♥6.

*346. If partner opens or overcalls 1♥ or 1♠ and later doubles 3NT, lead an unbid minor suit! Here's why: the normal lead is partner's major suit. If partner feels the hand will be defeated with the normal lead, partner passes. The double is to *divert* you from the normal lead. Partner has a two-suiter and wants you to find the second suit.

You hold: ♠84 ♥J10876 ♦84 ♣Q1062

(a) North	East	South (you)	West
1♠	1NT	Pass	3NT
Double	Pass	Pass	Pass

(b) West	North	East	South (you)
1♥	1♠	1NT	Pass
2NT	Pass	3NT	Pass
Pass	Double	Pass	Pass
Pass			

Partner wants a *minor* suit lead. From your hand, it looks like diamonds. Lead the ♦8.

347. After partner opens 1♣ or 1♦ and later doubles 3NT, the converse is true. There is a strong inclination to assume partner's minor suit opening is either short or weak after the opponents get to notrump. The double reassures you that it is not. Lead partner's suit!

You hold: ♠J1094 ♥J765 ♦8432 ♣2

North	East	South (you)	West
1♣	Double	Pass	2♥
Pass	2NT	Pass	3NT
Double	Pass	Pass	Pass

Lead a club, any club.

*348. If everybody bids a suit, consider suicide, but then lead dummy's first bid suit if it was bid at the *one level*. If dummy's first bid suit was at the *two level*, lead partner's suit.

East	South (you)	West	North
1♣	1♥	1♠	2♦
2NT	Pass	3NT	Double
Pass	Pass	Pass	

Partner wants a spade lead.

East	South (you)	West	North
1♥	1♠	2♣	2♦
2NT	Pass	3NT	Double
Pass	Pass	Pass	

Partner wants a diamond lead.

349. The double of a *voluntarily* bid suit slam, as opposed to a sacrifice, is similar to a double of 3NT; it asks for an unusual lead. If partner thinks the normal lead will defeat the slam, partner does *not* double.

350. There are certain leads that can be eliminated when partner doubles a voluntarily bid suit slam:

(1) A trump
(2) Any suit partner has bid
(3) The unbid suit — if partner has not bid.

351. The most common reason to double a slam is a void, particularly after a preempt.

You hold: ♠94 ♥32 ♦1087654 ♣QJ10

North	East	South (you)	West
4♥	4♠	Pass	4NT
Pass	5♥	Pass	6♠
Double	Pass	Pass	Pass

Partner probably has a diamond void with a side ace. A heart lead is out. Lead a diamond. Don't tell me you wanted to lead the ♣Q.

352. When a void seems remote, another possibility is that partner has an AK or AQ, usually in dummy's first bid suit. It is important to work out which is more likely, because if you don't, you will never hear the end of it!

353. A true masochist is one who doubles a suit slam with the AK of trump and then enjoys watching partner squirm while trying to work out the "killing" lead.

354. Trying to figure out which suit to lead vs. a doubled suit slam is akin to trying to figure out who the killer is in a movie mystery. In the movies, it's the butler; at the bridge table, it's usually the last suit you would have thought about leading.

355. The double of a notrump slam asks for the lead of dummy's first bid suit. Much easier.

CUEBIDS, CUEBIDS - Tips 356-367

356. Cuebids come in all shapes and sizes. They can:

(1) Show a control for slam purposes
(2) Show a two-suited hand
(3) Show a strong raise
(4) Create a force
(5) Ask for a stopper
(6) Show a stopper

357. After *major* suit *agreement* at the *three* level or higher, or after *minor* suit *agreement* at the *four* level or higher, new suits are slam-oriented cuebids.

(a) Opener	Responder	(b) Opener	Responder
1♦	1♥	1♣	1♦
3♥	4♣	3♦	3♥

In (a), 4♣ is a cuebid because there has been major suit agreement at the three level.

In (b), 3♥ is not considered a cuebid; it is an effort to get to 3NT. Here, the minor suit agreement came at the three level. It must come at the four level to be considered a cuebid. (See next tip.)

358. After minor suit agreement at the two or three level, new suits are considered efforts to get to 3NT - unless the subsequent bidding proves differently.

Opener	Responder
1♣	3♣
3♦	3NT
4♥	?

The 3♦ bid is considered a stopper-showing bid in an effort to get to 3NT. When responder bids 3NT and opener removes, all previous and subsequent bidding is slam invitational.

359. A cuebid in response to a major suit opening bid by an unpassed hand guarantees primary support and is a game force.

You hold: ♠AK87 ♥32 ♦KJ98 ♣Q98

North	East	South (you)	West
1♠	2♥	?	

Bid 3♥ to show primary spade support with an opening bid.

*360. A cuebid in response to a minor suit opening bid guarantees primary support plus an opening bid. It is forcing to 3NT or four of a minor.

You hold: ♠A76 ♥76 ♦KJ8 ♣KJ1076

North	East	South (you)	West
1♣	1♥	?	

Playing limit raises, this hand is too strong to bid 3♣. Bid 2♥, and see what happens. A good partner will turn up with a heart stopper. If you play forcing jump raises, respond 3♣.

Playing preemptive jump raises in competition, a cuebid is forcing to the three level of opener's minor.

361. A cuebid followed by a new suit is 100% forcing. No, make that 1000%.

You hold: ♠A ♥65 ♦A109876 ♣KQ105

West	North	East	South (you)
1♥	Double	2♥	3♥
Pass	3♠	Pass	4♦

The 4♦ bid, preceded by a cuebid, is forcing.

362. *Jump* cuebids show shortness plus primary support. Jump cuebids are game forcing and slam invitational.

You hold: ♠A76 ♥QJ876 ♦A876 ♣3

North	East	South (you)	West
1♥	2♣	?	

Bid 4♣, a splinter jump, impressing the whole table with your mastery of the latest gadgets. (Also, hope your partner knows what the h- - - you are doing.)

363. A direct jump cuebid in a *major* suit before partner has bid asks partner to bid notrump with a stopper in the opponent's suit.

You hold: ♠4 ♥A9 ♦Q104 ♣AKQJ876

East	South (you)
1♠	?

Bid 3♠, asking for a spade stopper. If partner doesn't have one, you will play the hand in clubs. A jump from one to three in the opponent's *minor* suit is natural.

364. After you, partner, and one opponent have bid and there has been no major suit agreement, a bid in the opponent's suit asks partner to bid notrump with a stopper in that suit.

You hold: ♠AJ4 ♥A109 ♦32 ♣KQ1087

South (you)	West	North	East
1♣	1♦	3♣	Pass
?			

You would like to play 3NT if partner has a diamond stopper. Bid 3♦ to ask. A good partner will have one.

365. If the opponents have bid two suits (as opposed to one), a bid in one of their suits shows a stopper and asks partner to bid notrump with the other suit stopped.

You hold: ♠A108 ♥A5 ♦87 ♣AKJ876

South (you)	West	North	East
1♣	1♠	2♣	2♦
?			

Bid 2♠ to show a spade stopper, at the same time asking partner to bid notrump with a diamond stopper.

366. When the opponents have bid one suit, a cuebid asks. When the opponents have bid two suits, a cuebid tells.

367. A cuebid at opener's first opportunity without suit agreement can be ambiguous. Opener can have one of two things in mind:

(1) Opener may have a fit for responder's suit.

(2) Opener may wish to ask for a stopper, holding a solid suit.

You hold: ♠A2 ♥AKJ4 ♦76 ♣AK876

South (you)	West	North	East
1♣	1♠	2♥	Pass
?			

Bid 2♠. When you later support hearts, your cuebid will be interpreted as a slam try.

You hold: ♠432 ♥4 ♦AK ♣AKQ8765

South (you)	West	North	East
1♣	1♠	2♥	Pass
?			

Bid 2♠! This time you are asking for a spade stopper. How will partner know? Partner will have to be patient. With a spade stopper, partner's *first obligation* is to bid notrump. If you later remove to hearts (see previous example), partner will know that the cuebid was based on a heart fit rather than a solid minor suit. As long as each of you knows the two possibilities, nothing too terrible can happen. (Send no letters.)

EVALUATING YOUR HAND - Tips 368-385

368. Do not be a slave to your point count. There are other, sometimes more important, factors to be considered.

369. Downgrade jacks and queens in suits bid by the opponents. *unless* partner makes a natural notrump bid. For example, you hold:
♠KJ4 ♥QJ87 ♦654 ♣1043

(a) | North | East | South (you) | West |
|---|---|---|---|
| 1♠ | 2♦ | ? | |

(b) | North | East | South (you) | West |
|---|---|---|---|
| 1♠ | 2♥ | ? | |

With (a), raise to 2♠. Your heart strength could be worth something. With (b), pass. Your heart strength is valueless on offense.

370. Avoid making any encouraging sounds with too much strength in the opponents' suit. Partner invariably thinks you have strength outside and bids too much. (See (b) in the previous tip.)

371. Downgrade honor cards in suits that have been bid to your *left*.

You hold: ♠KJ876 ♥AQ4 ♦KJ4 ♣32

South (you)	West	North	East
1♠	2♥	2♠	Pass
Pass	3♦	Pass	Pass
?			

Pass! Quickly! Your hand lost some of its value when West bid hearts. What little was left went down the drain when West bid diamonds.

372. Downgrade hands that have length in suits bid by the opponents, particularly your left hand opponent.

You hold: ♠AQ876 ♥AJ765 ♦K3 ♣3

South (you)	West	North	East
1♠	2♥	2♠	Pass
?			

Pass. What are you going to do with those hearts? If West had passed, you would have enough to bid on.

373. For notrump evaluation, downgrade hands lacking intermediate spot cards.

You hold: (a) ♠K43 ♥A2 ♦J543 ♣J876
(b) ♠K102 ♥A2 ♦J1054 ♣J987

Hand (a) counts out to 9 points; (b) is worth at least 10.

374. Add one point to any hand that has all of its strength in the two long suits.

You hold: (a) ♠K8765 ♥Q2 ♦KJ104 ♣Q5
(b) ♠AK876 ♥42 ♦KJ104 ♣32

Hand (b) is at least one point stronger than hand (a).

375. When considering a notrump bid, add one point for a five card suit headed by three of the top five honors.

You hold: (a) ♠K4 ♥AJ4 ♦K65 ♣QJ1076
(b) ♠K4 ♥AJ4 ♦K65 ♣AQ1076

With (a), bid as if you had 15 points; with (b), bid as if you had 18 points.

376. When faced with borderline decisions, let the strength of the intermediate cards in the long suit be the determining factor. Reread this one.

You hold: (a) ♠A86543 ♥K74 ♦KQ ♣Q3
(b) ♠AQJ1087 ♥AK4 ♦432 ♣2

South (you)	West	North	East
1♠	Pass	2♦	Pass
?			

With (a), bid a conservative 2♠.
With (b), bid an aggressive 3♠.

120

377. An ace and king in one suit is better than an ace in one suit and a king in another. This tip holds true for any two honor cards.

You hold: (a) ♠AK4 ♥654 ♦654 ♣KQ87
        (b) ♠A32 ♥K54 ♦K87 ♣Q765

Hand (a) is stronger than hand (b).

378. With 5-5 or 6-5 distribution, bid aggressively if your honor strength is concentrated in your long suits. Be careful if it is not.

You hold: (a) ♠AQ10543 ♥KQ954 ♦54 ♣-
        (b) ♠Q97654 ♥Q9654 ♦AK ♣-

Hand (a) is light years stronger than hand (b).

379. When an opponent shows a two-suiter, be leery of having your secondary honor cards in one of those suits ruffed away.

You hold: ♠KQJ ♥AJ987 ♦32 ♣QJ9

South (you)	West	North	East
1♥	1♠	2♥	Pass
Pass	3♦	Pass	Pass
?			

Be careful! East likes diamonds and probably has a singleton spade. If West realizes this and leads spades, you may not take many spade tricks. Your best bet is to pass.

380. When partner shows a two-suited hand, upgrade honor cards in partner's long suits as well as aces in the short suits. Downgrade secondary honors in partner's short suits.

You hold: (a) ♠Q4 ♥Q104 ♦A8765 ♣A109
        (b) ♠109 ♥Q4 ♦KQ1087 ♣KQ98

North	East	South (you)	West
1♠	Pass	2♦	Pass
2♥	Pass	2NT	Pass
3♥	Pass	?	

Hand (a) is enormous on the bidding; cuebid 4♣.
Hand (b) is worse; bid 3NT on the strength of your intermediates.

381. Long broken suits increase in value when (1) partner supports
the long suit; (2) partner is known to hold a balanced hand.

You hold: ♠QJ7643 ♥762 ♦K1064 ♣ −

(a) North	East	South (you)	West
1NT	Pass	?	

(b) North	East	South (you)	West
1♣	Pass	1♠	Pass
3♣	Pass	?	

In (a), your hand is easier to evaluate because you know partner has
at least two spades. Make an effort to get to 4♠.

In (b), you are in a quandary. If partner has a few spades, you have a
chance for game. If partner has a singleton spade, your hand is not
worth much. What should you do? If I knew, I would tell you.

382. Think in terms of tricks, not points, when holding an independent
suit (a suit that can play easily opposite a singleton).

You hold: ♠KQJ9874 ♥AKJ ♦43 ♣2

South (you)	West	North	East
1♠	Pass	1NT	Pass
?			

You have an independent suit. Count tricks! You have close to nine
tricks in your own hand − leap to 4♠. Bidding 3♠ is beneath
contempt.

383. Be patient when evaluating hands with singletons or voids. If
your shortness is partner's length, your hand loses value. If you have
support plus shortness, your hand increases in value. Patience.

You hold: ♠A876 ♥5 ♦KJ43 ♣8765

122

What is this hand worth? The truth is you can't tell until you hear the bidding. If partner bids spades, your hand is worth 11 points in support of spades. If partner bids hearts, you have an 8 point hand.

384. After you receive support and have a known *eight* card fit, use the *Rule of Seven* to determine just how much your hand has improved. What? You've never heard of the Rule of Seven? Of course you haven't; I just made it up.

You hold: (a) ♠AQ876 ♥KQ54 ♦A2 ♣54
(b) ♠AQ876 ♥KQ54 ♦A32 ♣5

South (you)	West	North	East
1♠	Pass	2♠	Pass
?			

After your suit has been raised and you are sure of an eight card fit but cannot be sure of a nine card or longer fit, add the length of your two longest suits (spades and hearts) and subtract seven from the total. Additionally, if you have a side singleton, add one extra point; with a side void, add two extra points.

Hand (a) increases in value by two points (subtract 7 from 9), and is now worth 17 points.

Hand (b) increases by three extra points because it has a singleton as well, and is now worth 18 points.

385. When you are assured of a nine card trump fit or longer, use the *Rule of Six*.

You hold: ♠AQ8765 ♥K4 ♦A876 ♣3

South (you)	West	North	East
1♠	Pass	2♠	Pass
?			

This time your hand increases by five points! Subtract six from the length of your two longest suits (spades and diamonds) giving you four extra points. You also have a side singleton, giving you one more point. Your 13 point frog has blossomed into an 18 point prince!

COMPETITIVE AUCTIONS - Tips 386-412

386. When the bid to your right is strong, a jump by you is weak.

East	South (you)
1NT (16-18)	3♦

1NT is strong, so 3♦ is weak.

387. When the bid to your right is *weak*, a jump by you is strong.

(a) East	South (you)
3♥	4♠(?)

3♥ is weak, so 4♠ is strong.

(b) North	East	South (you)
1♦	Double	2♥ (?)

Double is strong, so 2♥ is weak.

388. Anytime you are in a game-forcing auction and your right hand opponent intervenes, a pass by you is forcing.

You hold: ♠AQ76 ♥54 ♦K76 ♣QJ98

South (you)	West	North	East
1♣	Pass	2NT	3♥
?			

Pass. 2NT is a game force, so your pass is forcing. Maybe partner will have a better idea of what to do than you, for once.

389. Anytime you are in a game-forcing auction and your right hand opponent bids, a double is for penalty.

You hold: ♠AK765 ♥KQ5 ♦3 ♣Q987

South (you)	West	North	East
1♠	2♥	3♦	4♥
?			

Double. Even though a pass is forcing (see previous tip), your hand is suited to defense.

390. A raise in competition does not promise more than a raise made without competition; it simply denies a hopeless hand.

(a) **South** (you) **West** **North** **East**
    1♠   Pass   2♠   Pass

(b) **South** (you) **West** **North** **East**
    1♠   2♥   2♠   Pass

North does *not* show a stronger hand in (b).

391. Many competitive bids at high levels are made under pressure. As a result, you may not always have what partner expects, or vice versa.

You hold: (a) ♠KQJ10764 ♥3 ♦QJ5 ♣42
          (b) ♠KQJ107 ♥3 ♦QJ54 ♣J108

(1) **North** **East** **South** (you) **West**
    1♦   Pass   ?

With (a), respond 4♠.
With (b), respond 1♠.

(2) **North** **East** **South** (you) **West**
    1♦   4♥   ?

With (a), respond 4♠.
With (b), respond 4♠.

392. When there is little chance of getting doubled, bid close games vulnerable vs. not. Opponents tend to sacrifice. You might as well reap the profits.

393. Good players are loath to make low level penalty doubles without trump tricks. This means you can take liberties in low level competitive auctions with a strong suit.

394. As either opener or responder, after raising partner to the two level and hearing him pass, do not take the push to the three level with a balanced hand if the opponents compete. You either need a side suit singleton or undisclosed four card trump support.

You hold: (a) ♠4 ♥AK4 ♦A8765 ♣Q1043
         (b) ♠76 ♥AK42 ♦AQ87 ♣432
         (c) ♠64 ♥AK4 ♦AQ87 ♣7654

South (you)	West	North	East
1♦	Pass	1♥	Pass
2♥	Pass	Pass	2♠
?			

With (a), bid 3♣. You have a side suit singleton.
With (b), bid 3♥. You have undisclosed four card support.
With (c), pass. You have neither a side suit singleton nor a fourth trump.

395. When there is competition to your right which robs you of your normal rebid, pass with a minimum. Partner still has a chance to bid.

You hold: ♠87 ♥AK954 ♦87 ♣KQ87

South (you)	West	North	East
1♥	Pass	1♠	2♦
?			

Pass. If East had not bid , you would have rebid 2♣. However, you need extra strength to rebid 3♣, a new suit at the three level. No need to rebid hearts; partner already knows about that suit.

396. When there is competition to your right that does not rob you of your normal rebid, make it!

You hold: ♠AQ4 ♥AK876 ♦43 ♣432

South (you)	West	North	East
1♥	Pass	1♠	2♦
?			

You were going to raise to 2♠ without the 2♦ bid, so raise to 2♠ with the 2♦ bid.

397. Low level penalty doubles of suit contracts, or low level passes of partner's takeout doubles, are based on trump length and strength, *not* high card points.

398. It is easier to play a contract of 1NT than it is to defend one.

399. Be aggressive in the early stages of the auction. Bidding has a way of getting out of hand. Waiting in the bushes is for hunters, not bridge players.

400. After partner opens and second hand overcalls 1NT, double with 9 or more HCP. You have them out-gunned.

You hold: ♠AJ9 ♥32 ♦KJ976 ♣876

North	East	South (you)	West
1♥	1NT	?	

Double. Do not bid 2♦. (See next tip.)

401. After partner opens and second hand overcalls 1NT, bidding a new suit, jumping in a new suit, or jumping in partner's suit all show *weak distributional* hands. Your failure to double warns partner you are bidding on distribution, not strength.

You hold: (a) ♠54 ♥54 ♦QJ10876 ♣K54
           (b) ♠4 ♥54 ♦KQJ10876 ♣875
           (c) ♠3 ♥J1054 ♦K5432 ♣432

North	East	South (you)	West
1♥	1NT	?	

With (a), bid 2♦, not forcing.
With (b), bid 3♦, preemptive.
With (c), bid 3♥, preemptive.

402. Be familiar with the distinction between these two sequences:

(a) South	West	North	East
1♦	Pass	1♥	1♠
1NT			

(b)	1♦	1♠	Pass	Pass
	1NT			

In (a), opener shows 13-14 with a likely two spade stoppers.
In (b), opener shows 18-19, - a hand too strong to open 1NT.

403. There are 2NT rebids, and there are 2NT rebids.

(a) South (you)	West	North	East
1♥	2♣	2♠	Pass
2NT			

(b) South (you)	West	North	East
1♦	1♥	1♠	2♥
2NT			

In (a), your partner's response was at the two level in a *higher* ranking suit. Your 2NT rebid shows a minimum hand in the 12-14 HCP range.

In (b), you voluntarily bid 2NT after partner's one level response. You could have passed with a minimum. This 2NT rebid shows 18-19 HCP — as if East had passed.

404. A biggie: After you have limited your hand and your right hand opponent bids, unless you wish to make a penalty double, or have some unusual feature partner can't know about, it is almost always right to pass. Remember, you are limited so partner knows your hand better than you know partner's.

You hold: ♠AJ4 ♥KJ4 ♦KQ87 ♣QJ4

South (you)	West	North	East
1NT	Pass	Pass	2♥
?			

Pass. You have no surprises. Give partner a chance to do something intelligent. He may surprise you.

405. After either you or your partner has made a natural notrump bid, any double by either you or your partner is for penalty. Of course, there are two exceptions, both common expert practice.

(a) **South** (you)	**West**	**North**	**East**
1NT	2♥	Pass	Pass
Double			

(b) **South** (you)	**West**	**North**	**East**
1NT	3♣	Double	Pass

In (a), you have opened 1NT and your *left hand opponent* has over-called at the *two* level, passed back to you. A double in this sequence is considered a takeout double. It shows a small doubleton heart with a maximum 1NT opening bid. Had your right hand opponent over-called, double would be for penalty.

In (b), you have opened 1NT and your *left hand opponent* has over-called at the *three* level. A double in this sequence by your partner is considered to be the equivalent of Stayman. It is not a penalty double per se, although you are free to pass.

A possible South hand for (a) is: ♠A653 ♥43 ♦AKJ5 ♣AJ7
A possible North hand for (b) is: ♠AJ87 ♥KJ87 ♦654 ♣54

406. After a two level overcall, a 2NT response to an opening bid shows 10-12 HCP and is not forcing. With 13-16 HCP, respond 3NT.

You hold: (a) ♠A10 ♥KJ8 ♦Q987 ♣J943
          (b) ♠A10 ♥KJ8 ♦AJ76 ♣J943

North	East	South (you)	West
1♠	2♥	?	

With (a), bid 2NT.
With (b), bid 3NT.

407. The "death" distribution for competing in a major to the three level after partner has given you a single raise is 5- 3-3-2. Minimum hands with this distribution do better to defend rather than play at the three level.

You hold: ♠AQ987 ♥876 ♦QJ5 ♣A7

South (you)	West	North	East
1♠	Pass	2♠	3♥
?			

Pass. You have a minimum with the "death" distribution.

408. A delayed double by second hand when responder is *unlimited* and the opponents have *not* found a fit, is a penalty double.

You hold: ♠4 ♥AK1094 ♦KJ8 ♣A1042

East	South (you)	West	North
1♥	Pass	1♠	Pass
2♥	?		

Double - penalties! Responder is unlimited and the opponents have not found a fit.

East	South (you)	West	North
1♥	Pass	1♠	Pass
1NT	?		

Double - penalties. Responder is unlimited and the opponents have not found a fit.

409. A delayed double by second hand after the opponents have found a fit is a takeout double showing opening bid values.

East	South	West	North
1♥	Pass	1♠	Pass
2♠	Double		

Using the previous example hand, double 2♠ for takeout.

410. A delayed double after a 1NT response is for takeout if opener bids a new suit; for penalty if opener rebids the original suit.

(a) East	South	West	North
1♥	Pass	1NT	Pass
2♥	Double		

A penalty double. You could have the example hand given in tip 408.

(b) East	South	West	North
1♥	Pass	1NT	Pass
2♣	Double		

South holds: ♠AJ87 ♥K43 ♦K10842 ♣3

A takeout double. Responder has bid 1NT and opener has made a non-forcing rebid in a new suit.

411. Once you push the opponents to the five level, it is usually right to let them play there. After all, if they were happy to play at the four level, how thrilled can they be at the five level?

412. In a competitive auction, do not make a premature penalty double with an undisclosed fit for partner. First, show the support, then double if the opponents persist.

Both vulnerable, you hold: ♠A105 ♥KQJ ♦4 ♣A98765

West	North	East	South (you)
1♥	3♠	4♥	?

Don't double! Bid 4♠ and then double 5♥, if possible.

131

WHEN AN OPENING BID IS PASSED AROUND TO YOU - Tips 413-424

413. In the protective seat, you are allowed to bid with two points less than in the direct seat. Takeout doubles start as low as 9 HCP and simple overcalls at 7 HCP.

You hold: (a) ♠A987 ♥K543 ♦4 ♣Q765
(b) ♠Q10876 ♥AJ4 ♦43 ♣1087

West	North	East	South (you)
1♦	Pass	Pass	?

With (a), double.
With (b), bid 1♠.

Sitting North, pass the 1♦ opening bid with either hand.

414. If the opening bid is 1♣ or 1♦, reopen with 1NT holding 11-14 balanced. With 15-17, double and then bid 1NT.

You hold: (a) ♠AJ3 ♥Q104 ♦Q932 ♣A87
(b) ♠AK3 ♥K104 ♦Q932 ♣A104

West	North	East	South (you)
1♣	Pass	Pass	?

With (a), bid 1NT.
With (b), double and then bid 1NT.

415. If the opening bid is 1♥ or 1♠, reopen with 1NT holding 11-15 balanced. With 16-18, double and then bid notrump.

You hold: (a) ♠KJ76 ♥1087 ♦AJ ♣KJ54
(b) ♠KJ7 ♥A42 ♦AJ9 ♣KJ108

West	North	East	South (you)
1♠	Pass	Pass	?

With (a), bid 1NT.
With (b), double and then bid 2NT.

132

416. With notrump hands in the 19-20 range, bid 2NT immediately. With 21-22, double and then *jump* in notrump.

You hold: (a) ♠AK4 ♥K4 ♦AQ87 ♣A1052
(b) ♠AK4 ♥K4 ♦AQ87 ♣AQ105

West	North	East	South (you)
1♣	Pass	Pass	?

With (a), bid 2NT.
With (b), double and then jump in notrump.

*417. There is no such animal as the "unusual" 1NT in the balancing seat. 1NT shows 11/14-15 HCP, and 2NT, 19-20. With in between ranges, double and then bid notrump.

You hold: (a) ♠AJ4 ♥A1075 ♦K1076 ♣108
(b) ♠AJ42 ♥A10 ♦KQ86 ♣K106
(c) ♠4 ♥65 ♦AJ1054 ♣KQ1086

West	North	East	South (you)
1♠	Pass	Pass	?

With (a), bid 1NT.
With (b), double and then bid notrump.
With (c), bid 2♦; 2NT shows 19-20 balanced.

*A jump to 2NT by a *passed* hand in the balancing seat is unusual and shows a weak "freak" in the two lower ranking unbid suits.

418. Reopening with a cuebid shows a two-suited hand. Over 1♣ or 1♦, it shows the majors; over 1♥ or 1♠, it shows the other major plus an unspecified minor. (Partner bids 2NT to discover which minor.) The distribution is 5-5 or 6-5, and the range is 7-11 HCP. With stronger hands, bid your suits.

(a) West	North	East	South (you)
1♣	Pass	Pass	2♣ (majors)

(b) West	North	East	South (you)
1♥	Pass	Pass	2♥ (spades plus a minor)

419. Jump bids in the balancing seat are constructive, not weak. A jump in a suit shows a six card suit with 12-15 HCP.

You hold: (a) ♠AQJ876 ♥A54 ♦K4 ♣32
          (b) ♠AQJ876 ♥J54 ♦543 ♣2

West	North	East	South (you)
1♥	Pass	Pass	?

With (a), bid 2♠.
With (b), bid 1♠.

Sitting North, 1♠ with (a), 2♠, weak, with (b).

420. When a 1♣ opening bid is passed to you, keep in mind partner was not strong enough to overcall a measly 1♣ bid.

421. When a 1♣ opening bid is passed to you, check your club length. If you are short, partner may yet have a good hand. If you have club length, chances are partner is weak.

You hold: (a) ♠Q4 ♥876 ♦KJ76 ♣AJ97
          (b) ♠Q98 ♥A975 ♦KJ65 ♣74

West	North	East	South (you)
1♣	Pass	Pass	?

With (a), pass. Given your club length, partner is probably short in clubs and must be quite weak not to be able to make a peep at the one level. Opener probably has an 18-19 point balanced hand and is longing to get back into the bidding.

With (b), double. Your club shortness indicates partner may have a good hand with clubs after all.

422. When a minor suit opening bid is passed to you, be careful about reopening with a singleton in either major, particularly spades. The next thing you know, the opponents will find their fit.

You hold: ♠4 ♥AJ87 ♦KJ43 ♣10987

West	North	East	South (you)
1♦	Pass	Pass	?

Where are the spades? I'll let you in on a little secret; partner *doesn't* have them. Pass!

423. Reopening with a double jump shows a maximum preempt.

You hold: (a) ♠4 ♥AKJ10765 ♦Q76 ♣32
(b) ♠4 ♥QJ107654 ♦K54 ♣Q4

West	North	East	South (you)
1♣	Pass	Pass	?

With (a), bid 3♥, invitational. In this position, all jumps are invitational.

With (b), pass. Where are the spades? Bids of 2♥ or 3♥ are strength showing.

424. And the best for last: The jump cuebid. The jump cuebid shows a solid suit (usually a minor) and asks partner to bid notrump with a stopper in the opponent's suit.

You hold: (a) ♠42 ♥K4 ♦AKQ10876 ♣A8
(b) ♠K4 ♥42 ♦AKQ10876 ♣A8

West	North	East	South (you)
1♠	Pass	Pass	?

With (a), bid 3♠. A good partner will have a spade stopper. If not, you will play in diamonds.

With (b), bid 3NT. No, this is not a misprint. You are GAMBLING! Sometimes you have to. It's fun ... when it works! If they run the hearts, blame it on me. (You will anyway.)

WHEN THE OPPONENTS DIE OUT
AT THE TWO LEVEL - Tips 425-433

425. When the opponents give up the ship at the two level, you and your partner will have as many high card points as they will — at worst, it will be 22-18.

426. If the opponents have a known eight card fit and you have a singleton in their suit, double with as little as 8 HCP. With a doubleton, reopen with 10 + HCP.

427. Thou shalt not let the opponents play at the two level when they have a fit and you have shortness in their suit.

428. Fact: If the opponents have an eight card fit, your side also has an eight card fit (or longer) about 85% of the time. If the opponents have a nine card fit (or longer), your side will have at least an eight card fit 100% of the time. Bridge is a game of fits and misfits. You can take that statement any way you like.

429. A *reopening* bid in a suit is a desperation attempt to push them up one notch higher. With a good hand, you would have bid the suit one round earlier.

You hold: ♠A9854 ♥54 ♦K54 ♣432

East	South (you)	West	North
1♥	Pass	2♥	Pass
Pass	?		

Bid 2♠. They have an eight card fit and you have a five card major. Don't sell out. A good partner realizes that you were not strong enough to overcall 1♠ one round sooner. With a bad partner, it won't matter what you do.

430. A reopening bid of 2NT after the opponents have found a major suit fit is a minor suit takeout.

You hold: ♠4 ♥432 ♦KJ104 ♣AJ976

East	South (you)	West	North
1♥	Pass	2♥	Pass
Pass	?		

Don't sell out! Bid 2NT for the minors.

431. A reopening bid of 2NT after the opponents have *not* found a fit is natural. It shows 13-15 HCP and is definitely risky. However, the good news is you won't get your winners ruffed away in a crossruff.

You hold: ♠A76 ♥AJ8 ♦QJ76 ♣Q106

East	South (you)	West	North
1♦	Pass	1♥	Pass
2♦	Pass	2♥	Pass
Pass	?		

Try 2NT. Partner usually has a little something.

432. The real risk in reopening the bidding with a light hand is your partner. He invariably has 10-13 HCP and thinks he must tell you all about it. He forgets you are counting on him for that much. These partners must be trained. Read on.

433. The strategy behind balancing is to push the opponents to the three level. If you succeed, mission accomplished! Partner should not compete to the *three* level without primary support, a side singleton (or two side doubletons) and 12-15 support points. Reread this one.

Partner holds: (a) ♠A104 ♥32 ♦KJ87 ♣QJ32
(b) ♠A1042 ♥532 ♦K86 ♣A75
(c) ♠A1042 ♥3 ♦KQ987 ♣543

East	South	West	North (partner)
1♥	Pass	2♥	Pass
Pass	2♠	3♥	?

With (a) and (b), partner must be trained to pass.
With (c), partner is allowed to compete to 3♠.

REDOUBLES - Tips 434-439

434. When a one or two level takeout double made by your left hand opponent *has been converted to penalties,* "redouble" by either player is a cry for help.

You hold: ♠AQ4 ♥AK3 ♦8765 ♣987

South (you)	West	North	East
1♦	Double	Pass	*Pass*
?			

East's pass has announced strong diamonds. Unless you are a masochist of the highest order, you will not enjoy playing this hand in 1♦ doubled. Redouble for rescue.

435. A redouble of a takeout double *made by your right hand opponent* shows extras and is not a cry for help.

You hold: ♠AJ4 ♥65 ♦AKJ97 ♣AQ9

South (you)	West	North	East
1♦	Pass	Pass	Double
?			

Redouble to show 18+ HCP. Your redouble invites North to come back to the party.

436. These same principles apply after a one or two level overcall has been doubled for takeout and left in for penalties.

You hold: ♠ — ♥1086 ♦Q10976 ♣J10876

West	North	East	South (you)
1♥	1♠	Pass	Pass
Double	Pass	*Pass*	?

1♠ doubled does not look healthy. Redouble, asking partner to bid an unbid suit.

South holds: ♠AKJ875 ♥AQ4 ♦3 ♣Q105

East	South (you)	West	North
1♥	1♠	Pass	Pass
Double	?		

South redoubles to announce a powerful overcall. This double has not been converted to a penalty double.

*437. A pass after your right hand opponent redoubles varies in meaning with the level of the auction.

(a) West	North	East	South (you)
1♥	Double	Redouble	?

In this, the most common redouble sequence, a pass by you is non-committal, telling partner to bail himself out. It doesn't say that you have hearts.

(b) West	North	East	South (you)
3♥	Double	Redouble	Pass

After an opening *preempt*, followed by a takeout double and a redouble, "Pass" says that you want to play in 3♥ doubled and redoubled. In (b), you have hearts. Some play that pass is always non-committal after a redouble.

438. Assume you open the bidding, your left hand opponent doubles and partner redoubles. From that moment on, any subsequent double by either you or your partner is a penalty double — even at the one level.

You hold: ♠A54 ♥Q1097 ♦AK432 ♣2

South (you)	West	North	East
1♦	Double	Redouble	Pass
Pass	1♥	Pass	Pass
?			

Double. After a redouble by partner, tend to double any runout with four cards in their suit.

139

439. When your *right* hand opponent makes a strength showing redouble after having opened the bidding, "pass" by you is a penalty pass.

You hold: (a) ♠K54 ♥8765 ♦QJ4 ♣J87
          (b) ♠A2 ♥KJ987 ♦A1087 ♣109

East	South (you)	West	North
1♥	Pass	Pass	Double
Redouble	?		

With (a), bid 1♠. You do not wish to defend 1♥ redoubled.
With (b), pass. You would love to defend 1♥ redoubled.

WHEN PARTNER OPENS AND SECOND HAND DOUBLES - Tips 440-447

*440. A new suit at the one level is *unlimited* and forcing. If responder bids at the *one* level, it is as if the double never happened.

You hold: ♠4 ♥AJ1065 ♦KJ543 ♣Q3

North	East	South (you)	West
1♣	Double	?	

Bid 1♥. Do not redouble. With a five card major or a two-suited hand, bid your long suit at the *one* level if you can. Most experts use this method.

441. A *two* level response denies the strength of a redouble.

You hold: (a) ♠543 ♥2 ♦KQJ876 ♣1087
            (b) ♠543 ♥2 ♦KQJ876 ♣AQ8

North	East	South (you)	West
1♥	Double	?	

With (a), bid 2♦, not forcing.
With (b), redouble and then bid diamonds.

442. Most redoubles show balanced, or semi-balanced, hands with 11 + HCP. If partner opens 1♣ or 1♦, the redoubler should entertain some hope of doubling the opponents at a low level. If this is not the case, as responder start bidding your suits at the one level.

You hold: (a) ♠AK87 ♥43 ♦543 ♣KJ54
            (b) ♠KJ54 ♥AQ873 ♦5 ♣J76
            (c) ♠KJ94 ♥AQ93 ♦J1076 ♣9

North	East	South (you)	West
1♣	Double	?	

With (a), bid 1♠. This is not a hand where you are looking for a low level penalty double. This is a hand where you want to show partner spades and clubs. Your 1♠ response is unlimited and forcing.

With (b), bid 1♥. The opponents surely have a home in diamonds. Better to look for your own best contract before the diamond pre-empts start.

With (c), redouble. This is a defensive hand. The opponents may not have a home.

*443. With three card support for partner's major suit opening, raise to two with 5-8 HCP, *pass* with 9-10 HCP and redouble with 11 + HCP.

You hold: (a) ♠A87 ♥54 ♦J1087 ♣J543
(b) ♠A87 ♥54 ♦AJ54 ♣5432
(c) ♠A87 ♥54 ♦KQ87 ♣Q1087

North	East	South (you)	West
1♠	Double	?	

With (a), bid 2♠.
With (b), pass and then bid spades at your first opportunity (jumping in spades if partner bids in front of you).
With (c), redouble and then bid a minimum number of spades (11-12 HCP).

444. If you agree with the above tip, you will be involved in sequences like this with (b).

North	East	South (you)	West
1♠	Double	Pass	2♥
Pass	Pass	2♠	

This sequence shows a stronger hand than a direct raise to 2♠ but not quite strong enough to redouble.

North	East	South (you)	West
1♠	Double	Pass	2♣
2♥	Pass	?	

Bid 3♠. Partner has bid in front of you so jump to show 9-10 HCP.

445. With primary support for partner's major suit opening bid, you only have six ways to raise partner! You can raise to two, three or four; you can bid 2NT or 3NT, or you can redouble.

You hold: (a) ♠QJ54 ♥876 ♦K87 ♣876
          (b) ♠Q1087 ♥4 ♦K976 ♣8765
          (c) ♠J9765 ♥3 ♦K8765 ♣42
          (d) ♠AQ87 ♥54 ♦KJ43 ♣876
          (e) ♠AQ87 ♥54 ♦KJ54 ♣Q43
          (f) ♠AQ76 ♥A4 ♦KQ87 ♣876

North	East	South (you)	West
1♠	Double	?	

With (a), bid 2♠. A raise over a double is a weakness bid.
With (b), bid 3♠, preemptive.
With (c), bid 4♠, more preemptive.
With (d), bid 2NT, conventional and showing 10- 11 support points.
With (e), bid 3NT, 12-14 support points, equal to a forcing raise.
With (f), redouble, then jump to 4♠ (15-16 support points).

446. A jump bid is preemptive.

You hold: ♠KJ10876 ♥4 ♦J108 ♣1087

North	East	South (you)	West
1♦	Double	?	

Bid 2♠ to show a reasonable six card suit with 5-7 HCP. With stronger hands, bid 1♠, unlimited and forcing.

447. Redouble *promises* another bid if partner passes. You hold:
♠K4 ♥A987 ♦QJ87 ♣J87

North	East	South (you)	West
1♠	Double	Redouble	2♣
Pass	Pass	?	

Whatever you do, don't pass! Partner can have a whale of a hand, and you have given a blood oath to make another bid. Marriages have ended with South passing 2♣ in this sequence. Just kidding; only separations.

TWO-SUITED OVERCALLS - Tips 448-451

448. After a 1♣ or 1♦ opening bid, a cuebid of 2♣ or 2♦ shows 5-5 (or 6-5) in the majors with 7- 11 HCP. With 12-16 HCP, overcall in the higher ranking suit. With 17+ HCP, cuebid and then bid again after partner makes a minimum response.

You hold: (a) ♠AQ876 ♥K10954 ♦4 ♣54
         (b) ♠AKJ87 ♥KJ987 ♦3 ♣32
         (c) ♠AKJ87 ♥AKJ95 ♦4 ♣108

East	South (you)
1♦	?

With (a), bid 2♦.
With (b), bid 1♠. Too strong to bid 2♦.
With (c), bid 2♦ and then bid again after partner responds. (Concentrated strength is always worth at least one extra point.)

449. After a 1♥ or 1♠ opening bid, a cuebid of 2♥ or 2♠ shows five cards in the other major plus five or six cards in an unspecified minor (Michaels cuebid) 8-11 HCP or 17+ HCP. With 12-16 HCP, overcall 1♠ and then bid the minor at your next opportunity. (See tip #100.)

You hold: (a) ♠A10954 ♥4 ♦43 ♣KQJ87
         (b) ♠AQ987 ♥5 ♦43 ♣AQ1087
         (c) ♠AKJ87 ♥4 ♦K4 ♣KQJ65

East	South (you)
1♥	?

With (a), bid 2♥.
With (b), bid 1♠. Too strong to bid 2♥.
With (c), bid 2♥ and then bid again after partner responds.

450. After a 1♥ or 1♠ opening, a direct overcall of 2NT shows the minors (either 5- 5 or 6-5) with 8-11 HCP or 17+ HCP. With 12-16 HCP, overcall in diamonds and then bid clubs later.

You hold: (a) ♠5 ♥K4 ♦AJ1098 ♣QJ876
         (b) ♠5 ♥K4 ♦AQJ98 ♣QJ1087
         (c) ♠5 ♥K4 ♦AKJ98 ♣AQ1087

	East	South (you)
	1♠	?

With (a), bid 2NT.
With (b), bid 2♦. Too strong to bid 2NT.
With (c), bid 2NT and then bid again after partner makes a minimum response.

451. After a two-suited cuebid, the bidding may come up in such a way that partner does not respond. For example, your left hand opponent may bid. If the bidding comes back to you dead, pass with the 8-11 point hand, double with the stronger hand.

You hold: (a) ♠4 ♥K4 ♦AJ1098 ♣QJ987
          (b) ♠3 ♥K4 ♦AQ1098 ♣AKJ65

East	South (you)	West	North
1♠	2NT	3♠	Pass
Pass	?		

With (a), pass.
With (b), double to show a powerful two-suiter.

145

THE WEAK TWO BID - Tips 452-466

452. Think of a Weak Two as an opening three bid with one less card.

You hold: (a) ♠87 ♥AQ10732 ♦J54 ♣72
          (b) ♠87 ♥AQ10976 ♦J54 ♣76

With (a), open 3♥.
With (b), open 2♥.

453. There is no such animal as a Weak Two in clubs. 2♣ is reserved for all game-going hands and all balanced hands in the 22+ HCP range.

You hold: (a) ♠AKJ1087 ♥AK4 ♦AQJ ♣5
          (b) ♠KQ4 ♥AK65 ♦AK54 ♣K2

Open 2♣ with both of these hands. With (a), rebid 2♠.
With (b), rebid 2NT showing 22-24 HCP.

454. When you play Weak Twos, the 2NT opening bid shows 20-21 (or a flawed 22). A flawed 22 might have a doubleton KQ, KJ or QJ or 4-3-3-3 with no spot cards.

You hold: (a) ♠AJ8 ♥KQ43 ♦AK4 ♣K54
          (b) ♠KQ ♥AQ32 ♦KQ87 ♣KQJ

Open both hands 2NT. (Hand (b) is a flawed 22.)

*455. If you are lucky enough to be gazing at stronger balanced hands, open 3NT with 25-26; open 2♣ and rebid 3NT with 27-28 HCP.

You hold: (a) ♠AK4 ♥KQ87 ♦AJ ♣AKJ4
          (b) ♠AKJ ♥AKJ4 ♦AJ8 ♣AQ5

With (a), open 3NT.
With (b), open 2♣ and rebid 3NT.

Some play that an opening bid of 3NT shows a solid seven (or eight) card minor with no outside stoppers (Gambling 3NT). Others use the bid to show a solid minor suit (six or seven cards) with stoppers in at least two other suits (Strong Gambling 3NT).

456. 2♦ is an optional Weak Two. Some players use an opening 2♦ bid to show other types of hands - Flannery, etc.

457. Most Weak Two bids fall into the 6-9 HCP range; more important is the strength of the suit.

Vulnerable, the suit should have either three of the top five honors or two of the top five with the 9 and 8 thrown in for good measure. Not vulnerable, the 9 and 8 can be overlooked.

You hold: (a) ♠KJ8642 ♥K4 ♦762 ♣42
           (b) ♠KQ10763 ♥K4 ♦762 ♣42
           (c) ♠Q108765 ♥43 ♦AJ6 ♣64
           (d) ♠QJ9843 ♥43 ♦AJ5 ♣65

With (a), open 2♠ not vulnerable, pass vulnerable.
With (b), open 2♠ at any vulnerability.
With (c), open 2♠ not vulnerable, pass vulnerable.
With (d), open 2♠ at any vulnerability.

458. *Third seat* Weak Two bids can be opened with strong five card suits. Partner is a passed hand and must be trained not to tamper with third seat Weak Twos.

You hold: ♠43 ♥KQJ104 ♦K43 ♣987

North	East	South (you)	West
Pass	Pass	?	

Open 2♥ and join the world of thieves.

459. Fourth seat Weak Twos, as all fourth seat preempts, show super maximums. The range is 10-12 HCP.

You hold: ♠AK10543 ♥54 ♦QJ4 ♣J5

West	North	East	South (you)
Pass	Pass	Pass	?

Open 2♠. Partner will play you for something like this in fourth seat.

460. Do not open a Weak Two with a void. Partner assumes a *one* suited hand, and you may lose a fit in another suit.

You hold: ♠ — ♥AJ8765 ♦K432 ♣J54

Pass; it is anti-percentage to open 2♥.

461. Do not open a Weak Two in one major with four cards in the other major — unless your own major suit is independent. Never open 2♦ with a side four card major.

You hold: (a) ♠A1043 ♥A108432 ♦2 ♣98
          (b) ♠Q765 ♥KQJ1087 ♦43 ♣10

With (a), pass. If you open 2♥, you might miss a better fit in spades. With (b), open 2♥. Your hearts are so good that it won't matter if you miss a fit in spades.

462. Do not open a Weak Two with a side five card suit. (1) You may miss a better fit in your second suit. (2) Partner will not be able to evaluate his hand properly.

You hold: ♠4 ♥A108765 ♦K10876 ♣3

Pass; do not open this hand.

*463. It is permissible to open a vulnerable Weak Two with a solid six card suit and 6-3-2-2 distribution. Not vulnerable, partner will not play you for such a strong hand.

You hold: ♠AKQJ54 ♥54 ♦654 ♣32

Vulnerable, open 2♠. Not vulnerable, either pass or open 1♠, depending upon how light you and your partner open the bidding.

464. It is permissible to open a Weak Two with a side four card minor.

You hold: ♠AJ10543 ♥3 ♦Q1098 ♣32

Open 2♠ at any vulnerability.

465. In a competitive auction, the Weak Two bidder does not take the sacrifice. If a sacrifice is to be taken, it is partner who takes it. Reread this one. You hold: ♠5 ♥KQJ1043 ♦Q765 ♣32

Not vulnerable vs. vulnerable:

South (you)	West	North	East
2♥	2♠	4♥	4♠
?			

Pass. Partner knows the vulnerability and also knows more about your hand than you know about his.

*466. If partner responds 2NT, forcing, partner asks you to further describe your hand. You have some options. You can:

(1) Rebid your suit with a minimum.
(2) Raise to 3NT with a solid, or near solid, suit, i.e., AKJxxx.
(3) Show a side ace or king with a maximum.
(4) Jump to the four level in a strongish four card minor - if you have one.
(5) Jump to game with a strong suit plus a maximum plus a singleton.

You hold: (a) ♠QJ10543 ♥42 ♦AJ10 ♣87
          (b) ♠QJ10543 ♥42 ♦K76 ♣87
          (c) ♠AK10987 ♥2 ♦7654 ♣Q3
          (d) ♠A109876 ♥108 ♦KJ104 ♣3
          (e) ♠KQ9875 ♥10 ♦J876 ♣43
          (f) ♠AKJ976 ♥43 ♦876 ♣32

South (you)	West	North	East
2♠	Pass	2NT	Pass
?			

With (a), bid 3♦. Show the feature with a maximum.
With (b), bid 3♠ to show a minimum. No feature showing with minimums.
With (c), bid 4♠.
With (d), bid 4♦, showing a strong four card minor with a maximum.
With (e), bid 3♠, minimum.
With (f), raise to 3NT. You have a notrump spade suit.

Some play that a 2NT response asks for a singleton; others, for point count.

149

WHEN RESPONDING TO A WEAK TWO BID - Tips 467 - 472

467. You are facing a weak hand. Lacking support, you should be looking at 16 or more HCP to try for game. With a strong side suit, 15 HCP will do.

You hold: (a) ♠2 ♥AK543 ♦KQ87 ♣QJ3
          (b) ♠2 ♥AQJ987 ♦AK3 ♣J105

      North **East** **South** (you) **West**
      2♠   Pass   ?

With (a), pass. You don't have quite enough.
With (b), bid 3♥, forcing.

468. Assuming you have a strongish hand *without* a long suit of your own, the easiest way to find out about partner's hand is to make a forcing 2NT response. With a long suit and a strong hand, bid your suit. (See (b) in previous tip.)

You hold: (a) ♠87 ♥A987 ♦A87 ♣AK54
          (b) ♠K4 ♥AK87 ♦AK432 ♣87

      North **East** **South** (you) **West**
      2♠   Pass   ?

With (a), bid 2NT. If partner is minimum, give up on game.
With (b), bid 4♠. You have enough opposite a minimum without needing to ask.

469. A leap to 3NT ends the auction. Partner is not allowed to bid again.

You hold: ♠- ♥K43 ♦AKQJ876 ♣QJ9

      North **East** **South** (you) **West**
      2♠   Pass   ?

Bid 3NT and end the auction.

470. A raise is preemptive and partner is *not allowed* either to bid again or even think about bidding again!

You hold: ♠Q43 ♥43 ♦KQ87 ♣J987

North	East	South (you)	West
2♠	Pass	?	

Raise to 3♠. Make life miserable for them.

471. A double raise is a two-edged sword. It can be preemptive, or it can show a powerful hand that knows that slam is out of the question.

You hold: (a) ♠9 ♥K876 ♦K8765 ♣1087
(b) ♠AQ98 ♥105 ♦AK ♣A9876

North	East	South (you)	West
2♥	Pass	?	

Bid 4♥ with either hand. Let them worry about which one you have.

472. If you are incapable of passing 13-14 point hands with a singleton in partner's suit and no long suit of your own, do not play Weak Two bids!

You hold: ♠3 ♥AJ87 ♦KQ87 ♣KJ43

North	East	South (you)	West
2♠	Pass	?	

Pass with the speed of summer lightning!

WHEN THEY OPEN A WEAK TWO
Tips 473-479

473. Treat a Weak Two opening as a one bid. If you would double one, double two.

You hold: ♠A765 ♥54 ♦AK5 ♣J1087

East	South (you)
2♥	?

You would double 1♥, so double 2♥.

474. If they had opened one and you would have overcalled 1NT, overcall 2NT when they open two.

You hold: ♠AQ4 ♥KJ4 ♦QJ9 ♣AJ93

East	South (you)
2♥	?

If East had opened 1♥, you would have overcalled 1NT, so overcall 2NT over 2♥.

475. To overcall at the two level, you need either a strong five card suit with 12-16 HCP or a reasonable six card suit with 11-15 HCP. A three level overcall shows a strong six card suit with opening bid values.

You hold: (a) ♠KJ543 ♥A54 ♦65 ♣A76
(b) ♠KJ1042 ♥A76 ♦54 ♣A76
(c) ♠K109432 ♥AJ4 ♦K4 ♣65
(d) ♠54 ♥A87 ♦Q3 ♣KQ5432

East	South (you)
2♥	?

With (a), pass. Those spade spots make a two level overcall risky.
With (b), overcall 2♠.
With (c), overcall 2♠.
With (d), pass. No intermediates in your long suit.

*476. The next two tips are relatively new ideas: Cuebid their suit to ask for a stopper. The cuebid shows a solid minor, presumably with stoppers in the other suits. You hold: ♠K4 ♥54 ♦A3 ♣AKQ6543

(a) East	South (you)		(b) East	South (you)
2♥	?		2♠	?

With (a), bid 3♥, asking partner to bid 3NT with a heart stopper.
With (b), bid 3NT. No second choice.

*477. A jump to the four level in a minor shows that minor plus five cards in the other major. The distribution is either 5-5 or 6-5. The bid jump is invitational. It shows a very good hand. For example, you hold: ♠AQ1054 ♥2 ♦AKJ432 ♣2

East	South (you)
2♥	?

Bid 4♦, showing a diamond-spade hand needing very little for game.

478. With five or six cards in their suit, pass and hope partner can reopen with a double. You hold: ♠A4 ♥KQ987 ♦A4 ♣J876

East	South (you)
2♥	?

Pass — patience, patience, patience.

*479. With most minor two-suiters, bid 3♦ and then bid clubs. However, with an exceptionally powerful minor two suiter that wishes to play game regardless, make a jump cuebid.

You hold: (a) ♠3 ♥65 ♦AQJ87 ♣AQ1098
(b) ♠— ♥4 ♦KQ8765 ♣AK10876

East	South (you)
2♠	?

With (a), bid 3♦ and hope to bid clubs later.
With (b), bid 4♠. Using the jump cuebid to describe a powerful minor two suiter liberates a direct 4NT to be simple Blackwood.

CONVENTIONS TO BE FAMILIAR WITH
- Tips 480 - 495

480. **The Weak Jump Overcall:** The weak jump overcall shows the same type of hand as a weak two bid.

You hold: ♠KQ10876 ♥4 ♦QJ4 ♣432

East	South (you)
1♥	?

Bid 2♠. You would open this hand 2♠, so make a weak jump overcall with it.

481. Responses to a two level weak jump overcall are the same as responses to a weak two bid.

482. **Flannery 2♦:** An opening bid of 2♦ that shows five hearts, four spades and 11-15 HCP. With a stronger hand, open 1♥ and reverse into spades.

483. A reasonable defense to Flannery is to play:

(1) Double shows a balanced hand in the 13-15 HCP range.
(2) A 2NT overcall shows 16-18 balanced.
(3) A 2♥ overcall is for the minors.
(4) Overcalls of 2♠, 3♣ and 3♦ are natural.
(5) Jumps to 3♥ or 3♠ ask partner to bid 3NT with a stopper in that suit.

484. **Drury:** An artificial passed-hand response of 2♣ to an opening bid of 1♥ or 1♠. It asks whether the opening bidder has a real opening bid or has opened light to steal a partscore. Nine times out of ten, the Drury bidder has 10-11 HCP with three card support.

Playing Drury, you hold: ♠A87 ♥K3 ♦A765 ♣7654

South (you)	West	North	East
Pass	Pass	1♠	Pass
?			

Respond 2♣. In the most popular variation of responses to Drury, opener rebids the original suit with less than an opening bid and rebids 2♦ with a full opening or better. Jump rebids have specific meanings.

485. If the opponents use Drury, double 2♣ to show a club suit.

486. **The Responsive Double:** After partner makes a takeout double and third hand raises to two or three, double shows a balanced hand without direction. It is *not* a penalty double. The usual range is 7-10 HCP.

You hold: ♠A87 ♥5432 ♦K87 ♣Q87

West	North	East	South (you)
1♥	Double	2♥	?

Double to show high card strength *without* a long suit.

487. When *both* majors are unbid, a responsive double shows equal length in the majors, either three or four. With four cards in one major and three in the other, bid the four card suit.

You hold: (a) ♠K54 ♥A54 ♦8765 ♣J87
(b) ♠QJ54 ♥K543 ♦54 ♣J87
(c) ♠QJ54 ♥K53 ♦54 ♣J874

West	North	East	South (you)
1♦	Double	2♦	?

Double with (a) and (b). You have equal length in the unbid majors. With (c), bid 2♠.

*488. When one major suit is unbid, a responsive double leans toward the minors. If a responsive double is made with a four card major, the responsive doubler, *not the doubler*, is obligated to bid the major later.

You hold: (a) ♠987 ♥43 ♦AJ54 ♣K1065
(b) ♠43 ♥7532 ♦Q32 ♣AK87
(c) ♠43 ♥KJ987 ♦K54 ♣432

West	North	East	South (you)
1♠	Double	2♠	?

155

With (a), double. Perfect.
With (b), double and then bid hearts to indicate other possible trump suits in case partner has only three hearts.
With (c), bid 3♥. In this sequence, partner assumes five hearts (or four strongish hearts) because you didn't double and then bid hearts.

489. The Responsive Double after partner overcalls: After partner overcalls and third hand raises *beneath* game, double by fourth hand is takeout for the other two suits, usually 5-5, conceivably 5-4 with 8 + HCP.

You hold: (a) ♠K7532 ♥5 ♦AJ1084 ♣32
(b) ♠A9743 ♥92 ♦KQ75 ♣32
(c) ♠K43 ♥2 ♦Q432 ♣KJ1087

West	North	East	South (you)
1♣	1♥	2♣	?

With (a), double.
With (b), double.
With (c), pass. When you play responsive doubles, you can't change your system in midstream and make a penalty double.

490. Texas Transfers: When partner opens 1NT, a response of 4♦ is a transfer to 4♥; a response of 4♥ is a transfer to 4♠. This insures the hand is played by the notrump bidder.

You hold: (a) ♠AJ98754 ♥4 ♦543 ♣J10
(b) ♠54 ♥KJ98743 ♦QJ4 ♣3

North	East	South (you)	West
1NT	Pass	?	

With (a), respond 4♥ and pray your partner has not forgotten what you are playing.
With (b), respond 4♦ and keep praying.

491. Key Card Blackwood: In this variation, the trump king is counted as an "ace" or a key card. There are now five "aces" or five key cards.

You hold: ♠K4 ♥AJ1043 ♦KJ4 ♣432

	North	East	South (you)	West
	1♠	Pass	2♥	Pass
	3♠	Pass	4♠	Pass
	4NT	Pass	?	

The ♠K counts as an "ace" so you have two "aces" (key cards). Respond 5♥.

Responses are:
5♣ - 0 or 3 key cards
5♦ - 1 or 4 key cards
5♥ - 2 or 5 key cards
5♠ - 2 or 5 key cards with extras

492. **Roman Key Card Blackwood:** In this version, the responder counts both the king and queen of the agreed suit.

The responses are:
5♣ - 0 or 3 key cards
5♦ - 1 or 4 key cards
5♥ - 2 or 5 key cards without the queen
5♠ - 2 or 5 key cards with the queen

For practical purposes, the responder will not have five key cards. The player who asks for key cards is usually the stronger hand.

493. My preferred method of responding to Roman Key Card Blackwood is "**1430**" (Fourteen Thirty).

These responses are:
5♣ - 1 or 4 key cards (Fourteen)
5♦ - 0 or 3 key cards (Thirty)
5♥ - 2 without the queen
5♠ - 2 with the queen

This method is clearly superior when hearts is the agreed suit and the responder has one key card, a common situation. In this version, the response of 5♣ enables the key card asker to use 5♦ as an ask for the trump queen, eventually being able to play in 5♥ when the partnership is missing the trump queen.. In the original version, a 5♦ response shows one or four key cards, forcing the asker to bid 5♠ to inquire about the trump queen. If the responder does not have the trump queen, the partnership may be catapulted to an unmakable slam. If nothing else, play 1430 when hearts is the agreed suit, but my tip is to play 1430 ... period!

494. Jacoby 2NT Response: A 2NT response to a major suit opening bid shows a balanced game forcing raise. With visions of slam, opener makes a descriptive rebid.

495. Landy: When the opponents open 1NT, a 2♣ overcall is for the majors, typically 5- 5 or 6-5, with 9 + HCP.

496. A **Support Double** replaces the penalty double after partner makes a one level major suit response and your right hand opponent overcalls or raises partner's overcall beneath the two level of responder's suit.

You hold: (a) ♠A2 ♥K76 ♦AQ765 ♣432
(b) ♠A2 ♥K764 ♦AQ765 ♣32
(c) ♠4 ♥K76 ♦AKJ87 ♣AJ92

South (you)	West	North	East
1♦	Pass	1♥	1♠
?			

With (a), double, conventional (support double), showing a heart raise with three card support.

With (b), bid 2♥. When playing support doubles, the direct raise over interference shows four card support and is limited to a minimum hand.

With (c), double and then bid 3♣ (if partner bids 2♥) to complete the picture of your hand.

If your right hand opponent intervenes with a natural 1NT overcall, support doubles are off. A double by the opener is a penalty double.

WHAT'S LEFT - Tips 495 - 540

495. Opponents who bid to the heavens vulnerable vs. not with limited high card strength invariably have wild distribution.

496. With nine winners in your own hand, plus an independent major suit, bid game. Do not invite. A good partner will give you the tenth trick.

You hold: ♠AKQJ87 ♥KQJ ♦A105 ♣7

East	South (you)	West	North
1♦	Double	Pass	1♥
2♣	?		

Jump to 4♠. Do not invite with 3♠.

497. If you are playing bridge with your husband, your wife, or your significant other, don't.

498. A 4-4 trump fit *usually* plays at least one trick better than a 5-3 trump fit.

West (you)	East
♠AQJ4	♠K876
♥AQ1054	♥KJ9
♦A2	♦543
♣A2	♣543

In a contract of 6♠, all you need a 3-2 trump division. You can discard two of dummy's diamonds (or clubs) on your hearts and eventually ruff a diamond. You lose one club. In a contract of 6♥, you can stand on your head, but you will still lose one club and one diamond.

499. A 4-4 trump fit *usually* plays at least one trick better than a notrump contract.

West (you)	East
♠KJ109	♠AQ42
♥A87	♥43
♦KJ10	♦AQ87
♣K87	♣A42

6♠ is ice cold. 6NT has no play. Notice that there are 31 HCP between the two hands. With a 4-4 trump fit, 31 or 32 HCP between the two hands is usually enough to make slam. Of course, it helps to have a strong trump suit and controls.

500. *Their* bidding often gives you the key to partner's distribution. This, in turn, can make your bidding more accurate.

You hold: ♠7654 ♥AKJ98 ♦AQ4 ♣3

South (you)	West	North	East
1♥	1♠	2♥	2♠
?			

It doesn't take Einstein to figure out that partner is short in spades. Your hand is better than it looks. Either make a game try with 3♦ or bid 4♥. Do not make the all time wimp bid of 3♥.

501. The right bid with one partner may well be the wrong bid with another. Reread this one.

502. If you find yourself losing your hair when partner plays the hand, bid notrump sooner.

503. Partner is more apt to stay the course if he knows your distribution as opposed to your point count.

504. Give up on fancy bids with weak partners. They figure to backfire.

505. More points at the bridge table are lost through cowardice than recklessness. It's a bidder's game.

506. There isn't room at the table for four good hands. If everyone at the table is bidding his head off, someone is lying. Let's hope it isn't you!

507. The greatest show of willpower on earth is not to mention to partner an obvious error. Repeated demonstrations of this may qualify you for sainthood and ulcerhood.

508. If you really want to improve your bridge, play with and against good players. Too many things work against weak players. You cannot improve your game under those circumstances.

509. When you and your partner adopt a convention, be prepared for interference and decide how to handle it.

510. With a *weak* hand and a choice of bids, one limited and one unlimited, make the limited bid.

You hold: ♠KQ87 ♥J104 ♦32 ♣J1043

North	East	South (you)	West
1♥	Pass	?	

Your choices are 1♠, unlimited, or 2♥, limited. Bid 2♥.

511. With a new partner, the fewer conventions the better. You'll both be more relaxed.

512. If your partner appears uncomfortable with a certain convention, don't play it. Chances are it won't come up anyway.

513. When you have a choice of sensible bids, make the one that pays off the most if it works.

514. System cannot replace judgement. Nothing can.

515. They say you can't have good sex with your partner after a bad game. Just kidding. I wanted to see if you were still awake.

516. Let the opponents make the "genius" bids. Keep yours down to a minimum. Partners never seem to work them out.

517. Do not bid a grand slam in notrump unless you can count thirteen tricks. Do not bid a suit grand slam unless you have solid trumps between the two hands, as well as thirteen tricks, counting ruffs and/or long suit establishment. No grand slams on finesses!

518. Always consider what partner has *not* bid.

West	North	East	South (you)
1♣	Pass	2♣	?

Partner wasn't able to overcall 1♦, 1♥ or 1♠.

519. A partner who passes over an opposing opening bid and then comes to life later usually is well stacked in opener's first suit.

West	North	East	South (you)
1♣	Pass	Pass	1♥
Pass	3NT		

North has a strong hand with clubs.

520. If partner says he enjoyed playing with you after you've had a bad game, he's probably lying.

521. Do not let bad results get to you, — or worse, let partner see that they have gotten to you. Assume things will turn around; they usually do.

522. A simple "nice bid" to partner goes a long way in cementing a partnership.

523. If you don't want to get doubled, bid in a confident tone. The opponents will be impressed, and so will partner.

524. Don't be afraid to bid against experts. That's one reason they win so often — opponents are beaten before they get to the table. Also, experts don't like defending against preempts any more than you do.

525. In most sequences, there is a captain and a private. The private is the first player to limit his hand. The troublesome sequences are the ones where neither hand is limited and there are no captains, — or worse, one captain and one general!

526. As the auction continues, ask yourself what your partner already knows about your hand. Do not tell the same story twice. Assume partner is not hard of hearing.

527. It is easy to envision the perfect hand partner might have to make your overbidding look good. Partner *never* has that hand.